Copy that!

Boost your translation or freelance business by offering copywriting as a service

Antoinette Chappell

Copyright © Antoinette Chappell 2023. All rights reserved.

This book or any portion thereof may not be reproduced or used in any manner whatsoever without the express written permission of the publisher except for the use of brief quotations in a book review.

Strenuous attempts have been made to credit all copyrighted materials used in this book. All such materials and trademarks, which are referenced in this book, are the full property of their respective copyright owners. Every effort has been made to obtain copyright permission for material quoted in this book. Any omissions will be rectified in future editions.

Cover image by: Diocebel Aballa, 99D
Book design by: SWATT Books Ltd

Printed in the United Kingdom
First Printing, 2023

ISBN: 978-1-7390884-0-8 (Paperback)
ISBN: 978-1-7390884-1-5 (eBook)

ARC Writing and Translation Services
London

info@arc-wts.co.uk

Dedication

To my children, Bradley and Jasmine, so that you may have the courage to follow your heart, realise your dreams and ignore the naysayers, of whom there will always be many.

Contents

This book is for you if: 11
Foreword 13
Acknowledgements 15
Introduction 17

Part one   *19*

Chapter 1: What is copywriting? 21
    Why did I become a copywriter? 22
    What does a copywriter do? 23
    Don't waffle! 24
    What skills make a good copywriter? 25

Chapter 2: Transferable skills 33
    Skills translators and copywriters have in common 34
    Six key transferable translating skills 34

Chapter 3: Overcoming your fears 45
    Starting with a blank page 46

Chapter 4: Owning it! 51
    Reinventing yourself and believing it 52
    Say it and it will happen! 52
    Complete a copywriting course 53
    What to look for in a copywriting course 54
    Face-to-face networking 54

Hire a coach or mentor 55
Ignore the naysayers 55
Tasks to complete 57

Part two   *59*

Chapter 5: Getting started 61
Passive steps 62
Active steps 70
Tasks to complete 74

Part three   *75*

Chapter 6: The art and science of copywriting 77
Know your audience 78
Who are you talking to? 79
Determining a client avatar 80
Gathering psychographic information 80
Outline your buyer persona's typical day 81
Copy strategy: identifying the purpose of the copy 82
Tone of voice 83
What is 'tone of voice'? 84
List of detailed tone descriptors 84
What do you want the reader to do after reading the copy? 85
What language does your reader use? 85

Chapter 7: Ripping up the rules 87
Ripping up the rules: time to forget grammar 88
When else can you forget grammar in copywriting? 89
Welcome to AIDA 89
Keywords and why they matter 93
Writing a brief 94
What to include in your brief 94
Crucial differences between copywriting and translating 96
Tasks to complete 97

Part four   *99*

Chapter 8: Ready to launch 101
   Launching as a copywriter 102
   How to find your first client 102
   B2B or B2C 103
   Social media marketing 104
   Which platform is best for you? 104
   Digital marketing 105
   Referral marketing through networking 106
   Asking for testimonials/reviews 106
   Identify your brand 107
   Develop your pricing structure 107
   Productise your services with packages 108
   The importance of building a portfolio 109
   Using consistent messaging 110
   To niche or not to niche? 110
   Using humour in copy 112
   Managing your first client 113
   What to talk about on a discovery call 113
   This is how I structure my discovery calls: 114

Chapter 9: The customer is not always right 117
   Dealing with a dissatisfied customer 118
   What can go wrong in copywriting 118
   What to do when writing copy for a third party 121
   New client questionnaire 122
   The brief is so important! 130
   Tasks to complete 131

Part five   *133*

Chapter 10: How to network 135
   Networking: how to do it right 136
   How not to network 136
   My path to getting it right 136

My first networking meeting 137
A steep learning curve 138
Know, like and trust 138
Exploring different networking groups 139
Different networks you should join 140
Networking in your industry 141
Networking in your ideal client's industry 141
Networking with other business owners 142
How to get maximum value from networking 142
Different forms of networking 146
Ideal referral partners and how to identify them 147
Non-referral networking 147
Teams that serve the same clients 148
Who should you book one-to-ones with? 148
LinkedIn: the world's largest business network 149
How to make LinkedIn work for you 149
Key reasons to network 150
What makes a good networker? 151
What to include in your pitch? 151
Final note on networking 154
Difference between networking groups and conference networking 155
Tasks to complete 157

Part Six   *159*

Chapter 11: Copywriting and AI: what the future holds 161
ChatGPT: my initial introduction 162
Creative destruction: what is it? 163
AI and its impact on translation 165
AI and its impact on copywriting 166
Using AI chatbots as productivity tools 170
What is prompt engineering? 170
Who AI-generated copy works well for 172
How to edit AI-generated copy 172
Potential legal ramifications of using AI-generated content .. 173
Final thoughts on AI 174

Chapter 12: Cha-ching **177**
    Managing two arms of your business 178
    Watch the money roll in 179
    You determine your own level of success 180
    Tasks to complete 182

Final words 183
About the author 185
Recommended reading 187
Bibliography 189
Endnotes 191

COPY THAT!

This book is for you if:

- You are a translator looking to add another income stream
- You are a freelancer with strong writing skills and would like to add copywriting as a service
- You are a technical writer and would like to find out more about writing to sell
- You run a small business and would like to improve your copywriting skills for social media posts
- You are a small business owner and would like to improve your copywriting skills to write more engaging blogs
- You run your own business and would like to know more about networking
- You work in digital marketing and would like to improve your copywriting skills
- You run a marketing team and would like to improve your team's copywriting abilities
- You love writing and want to start offering copywriting as a service

COPY THAT!

Foreword

This book is a wonderful reflection of the journey I have seen Antoinette take, transitioning from a translator who rarely had any verbal or in-person contact with her clients, when I first met her, to the busy outgoing copywriter she is now, with a flourishing London-based business.

Antoinette was a client of mine who I coached for about 18 months from 2019 to 2020. During the time that we worked together, I witnessed her transform from someone who was stuck and couldn't see a way forward to someone who is thriving professionally.

As I read this book cover to cover, I took a trip down memory lane and flashed back to conversations we had had, often in high-end coffee shops in Brighton, exploring various mindset and business issues. In part through our coaching sessions, Antoinette has overcome her false and self-limiting beliefs and challenged her assumptions. She now shares her wisdom and experience in this book to help others who face similar challenges, whether they are in the translation industry specifically or a self-employed person in another field who wants to grow their business and market their services more effectively.

Having hired several copywriters over the years, I have personally never worked with a copywriter whose work needs so little tweaking. Antoinette regularly writes blogs and landing pages for my business and for my clients. I have always been extremely impressed with the high standard of her work and how she can expertly craft copy that accurately conveys my message. Her lifelong passion for languages and commitment to flawless writing and clear messaging makes her the ideal person to write a book about her copywriting journey to assist solo entrepreneurs who feel stuck, lonely in business and unable to see a pathway forward.

What struck me when I read this book was how much Antoinette would have benefited from it when she set off on her journey to add copywriting as an additional service. I think it is a godsend for translators who feel stuck in their business and want to explore ways to move forward by leveraging their existing excellent writing skills. Therefore, I highly recommend this book to translators who want to find out how to add another income stream by using the transferrable skills they already possess. This is also a very useful read for self-employed people interested in how to network more effectively and pivot their businesses successfully.

This book is not a manual on copywriting, but a valuable source of information that can help any small business owner grow and expand their business. For example, it contains detailed advice on how to use networking to grow your business and develop as a business owner. In many respects, I consider it a guide to running and developing a small business, and it reflects many of the business coaching conversations I have with my clients. In my opinion, the contents of this book represent a valuable tool for business owners who want to diversify their range of services, change their mindset and effect positive change without or perhaps in addition to hiring a business coach.

Jason Cornes, Business & Executive Coach
www.jasoncornes.co.uk

Acknowledgements

Like any author, I owe a debt of gratitude to all the people who helped me get this book over the line and become a tangible reality. I will start by thanking my book writing coach Georgia Varjas who initially inspired me to write the book, encouraged me throughout the writing process, held me to account and provided constructive feedback and insights during the time we worked together.

I'd also like to thank my husband, James, who is my rock and allowed me the time and space to write this book and offered his continuous and steadfast support and never once doubted my ability to write this book. I'd like to thank my brother, Stephen Moore, for his unwavering support and for not once questioning my decision to write it. I'd also like to thank my children, Bradley and Jasmine, my stepsons Calum and Conor, my grandson, Vinnie, and my step-grandchildren Addie and Greyson, for giving me a reason to write it to create a lasting legacy as well as set an example to them that you must always follow your dreams and believe in yourself. I'm also eternally grateful to my parents, Ann and Roger Moore, for the love, encouragement and opportunities that they have unconditionally given me my whole life.

Thank you also to my business coach, Jason Cornes, whose expert guidance and advice helped me to overcome my false and self-limiting beliefs and enabled me to transform myself from a shy introverted translator to a confident, socially extravert copywriter.

Lastly, thank you Annabel Tiplady for unknowingly providing inspiration for the book. My determination to help newly qualified and seasoned translators and other business owners navigating today's fast-moving business landscape by creating a portfolio business was sparked by our first meeting.

Introduction

They say everyone has book in them and, in my case, I always knew that was true, but it was more of a feeling and a passion for writing than a clear story with a narrative that would interest and engage readers. Originally, I always thought I would write a fiction book, and I may well do one day, but this first book came about almost by accident. Are you sitting comfortably? Good, then I'll begin.

As an avid networker, one of the people in my sphere of contacts was Georgia Varjas. Georgia is a highly experienced book writing coach whose exuberance and can-do attitude is incredibly motivating and infectious. I knew Georgia vaguely from a few online meetings and from following her on social media. I was interested in her book writing coaching service and wondered if she could help me write my first book and, crucially, decide what to write about, so I registered for one of her free webinars.

One cold evening in November 2022, the day of the webinar arrived, and I logged in not really knowing what to expect but keen to find out more. On the call, there were about ten or so people, mostly all at the beginning of their book writing journey, who wanted to find out more about how to get started and what it would be like working with Georgia.

All the attendees shared their book ideas and one thread that seemed to run through their ideas was writing about your own experiences to help others in a similar situation. This really struck a chord with me. I had never considered writing a book that could help others before and this got me thinking, "What knowledge do I have that could help other people in a similar situation to me?". This question of whom I could help sat in my mind, and then the answer came to me like a revelation. I realised that all the knowledge I had accrued over the past few years in terms of learning to network and copywrite and, more recently, using AI to improve my workflow, could help other translators who may also want to create a new income stream via copywriting.

Enter Annabel Tiplady...

Not long after that, I recalled a Zoom meeting I had had a few months previously with Annabel Tiplady, a young translation graduate who was rather disheartened with the way the translation industry was heading with the increased use of AI, not to mention the extremely tight deadlines that continue to be commonplace in the industry. Annabel had mentioned an interest in the copywriting coaching service that appeared on my website, but I hadn't really promoted it or got it off the ground. I felt like I wanted to help Annabel, but I didn't really feel I had any relevant resources or a place to direct her to in order to help her to explore other professional avenues.

Then, one day, the idea came to me. I will write a book that can help translators who want to become copywriters. I will share everything that I have learnt so that they can avoid some of the mistakes I have made along the way and benefit from my experience and successes.

So that is what I set out to do and that is what I hope I have achieved. This book is *not* a copywriting manual; there are plenty of those on the market. This book is intended to be a guide and a toolkit that translators, other language professionals or business owners can dip into to see what it takes to be a copywriter. Then, how to market yourself as a copywriter, pivot your business, network successfully, and harness AI to speed up your workflow. All this leads to the concluding stage: how to create a successful portfolio business.

I hope you find it useful for your own business or professional journey.

Part one

COPY THAT!

Chapter 1
What is copywriting?

Parla bene, ma parla poco
(Speak well, but speak little)

If you're reading this book, I am guessing that, if you are a translator, you are interested in finding ways to enhance and develop your business. Perhaps you would like to create another income stream for your business to supplement your translation work. Maybe you want to start offering transcreation as an additional service. Transcreation, for those of you not familiar with this rather awkward hybrid term, is a blend of translation and creation. It goes beyond pure word-for-word translation, to adapt and interpret the meaning of text while maintaining its style, intention, tone and context. Or it could be that you need to promote your own translation business better by learning how to write in a way that engages and resonates with your ideal client. This book aims to cover all these topics.

If you're not a translator this book can help you find out what it takes to be a copywriter and how to start.

Whatever your reason for being here, it's important from the outset that you have a clear understanding of what copywriting is and the purpose it serves. Many people get confused between copywriting and copy editing and some even confuse it with copyright, which is an intellectual property right.

Why did I become a copywriter?

Back in 2019, after having been a freelance translator for 12 years, I hired a business coach to shake up my business and help me to find another service I could offer using the skills I had. At that time most of my translation clients were translation agencies, and post-editing machine translation (PEMT) was becoming more prevalent and was less lucrative than human translation.

As adoption of PEMT increased across the board, I could foresee a downward trajectory in my income in the coming years, coupled with a rise in tedious post-editing work that mainly comprised formatting numbers, spotting and correcting errors and the kind of mistakes only machine translation could make. A good example of this is translating people's names, so "Pietro" becomes "Peter" for example.

After taking a deep dive into my core skills and having carried out personality and strengths assessments, we identified copywriting as a service I could offer. Great, I thought, but where do I start and how do I find clients?

If, right now, you are asking yourself those same questions, read on! As you go through this book you will learn the story of the journey I went through to become a competent freelance copywriter, from my very first task to the kind of clients I now work with. Boy, I wish I'd had a similar book to hand to guide me in 2019!

What does a copywriter do?

A copywriter writes original, creative content for a specific audience that ensures brand consistency. It's a critically important component of advertising and marketing; think of the words you read on any advert, website or app. Have you ever wanted or needed a product and felt an advert you read or listened to was talking directly to you? That's what good copywriting feels like. It has been written to appeal to people like you with your particular interests, tone of voice, needs, wants and desires.

Conversely, how many times have you read or listened to an ad and thought "Who would want to buy that?" That is either because it is not targeted at you or it has not been written in a way that understands its potential audience.

Copywriting is often used to sell a product or service directly through an advert. However, that sales process is now often conducted in a more subtle way. Copywriting is at the heart of selling by educating, entertaining and informing people about a product or service. There are now so many different types of media which can be used for this. It could be an article on LinkedIn, a blog or podcast, or a simple brochure. These all have different intended uses, and the copywriter needs to write copy which matches the style of selling and the medium being used.

You may have heard of copy editing, which is a different skill. So, it is necessary at this stage to highlight the differences between copywriting and copy editing. A copy editor edits a copywriter's work, ensuring it is accurate, both grammatically and factually, and hits the right tone. A copy editor has the job of reviewing and refining a text to ensure accuracy, clarity, coherence and adherence to style guidelines. They work on various types of written material such as articles, manuscripts, reports, marketing materials, etc.

Don't waffle!

In copywriting it is crucial to be succinct, to the point and target the right client avatar. A client avatar is your ideal client narrowed down to one person who you can assign a name to. When you are writing copy you can then keep them in mind and imagine that you are talking directly to them. I have described how you identify your client avatar in more detail in Chapter 6. Delivering on your client's brief as concisely as possible is key to crafting copy that hits the spot and persuades the reader to act. That action could be, in a sales context, clicking 'Buy now' or 'Contact us' on a website. In a recruitment situation, it could mean helping someone to decide that they want to work for a particular company because how you have described their values and how they treat their staff is exactly what they are looking for in an employer.

What skills make a good copywriter?

To be a good copywriter, you need to be competent in the following:

- Research
- Excellent command of the language you are writing in
- A good ear for the tone of voice required
- Client and audience empathy
- Ability to collaborate
- Ability to communicate
- Project management
- Creativity/ideation
- The confidence to be bold in your writing

As with all professions, you need to have a set of complementary skills to be able to be good at what you do. Let's now look at why you need all or some of the skills above to be a successful copywriter.

Research

Copywriters often work as freelancers and tend to work for a variety of different industries, especially in the beginning before they have established a niche. You probably did the same when you started your translation career, unless you came from another industry first, engineering, or the legal or medical profession, for example. Either way, you will need to research the industry your client is in; even if it is an industry you are familiar with, you need to keep abreast of the latest industry trends and developments and what your client's competitors are doing.

In fact, as a copywriter, you will need to dedicate time to following your client's competitors, especially those that your client is most keen to emulate or outperform. The best way to do this is to follow them on social media and visit their website regularly to read their latest news or blog posts.

I was recently hired to write the website copy for a large group of facility management companies that had recently lost out on a major project they had tendered for to a rival competitor. When they asked the client why their bid had been unsuccessful and for feedback they were told the competitor had more to offer than they did. When pressed for which additional services their competitor offered specifically, the client could not identify any. The only difference between them was their websites. The competitor had a brand new, fresh, people-centric website that focused on highlighting its commitment to sustainability, diversity and inclusion, thus creating the (real or perceived) impression of added value.

My client understood that their tired, traditional website was holding them back and costing them clients and that something had to change. To remain competitive, they had to improve their marketing and this started with a new website. My task was to write copy for their new website that was even better than their competitors so that they didn't lose the next tender due to a perceived difference between them and their main competitor.

The website is now live and performing well, and since it went live, they haven't lost any tenders. Their website now creates the correct impression of them being on-point, progressive and leading the way in their industry.

Excellent command of the language you are writing in

As a translator, it is my job to ensure that every translation I deliver reads fluently in the target language and is correctly localised, which in my case means British English. So, I root out U.S./International English spelling conventions such as *"labor" "center"* or *"color"* or grammatical mistakes. This also applies to copywriting.

Although you can bend the grammar rules more in copywriting (see Chapter 7 for more details about this), this should only be done to create a particular effect and not because of incompetence or a lack of knowledge and understanding of the grammar of the language you are writing in. This is one key area in which the written skills you have acquired over the years you have spent translating can be repurposed for copywriting.

A good ear for the tone of voice required

Developing a skill for listening to the language the client avatar for your copy uses in their everyday speech and then replicating this is essential to resonate with the intended audience for the copy. You can do this by accessing the same media as the client avatar you are writing for. For example, if your client avatar is a 30-year-old British female leadership coach, you could access articles online or on LinkedIn from financial publications such as Forbes. If you go to the person's profile you can see who and which publications they follow.

You could also search people on LinkedIn whose job title is 'Leadership coach' and then follow any female coaches and see what kind of language they use in their posts and what their peers say in the comments. You could also visit their website and/or search 'female leadership coach' on YouTube and watch some videos, again to access the tone of voice that they use when communicating about their work. See Chapter 6 for a more in-depth explanation about how to establish the correct tone of voice.

Client and audience empathy

Empathy is an essential attribute for any copywriter. Why, you might ask. Well, because in order to write copy that the reader feels is talking to them you need to get inside their head, feel their pain and understand why the solution you are proposing with the product or service you are promoting is the answer their problems.

Without going into detail about the neuroscience behind why people buy and what influences their buying decisions, as that is not the purpose of this book, suffice to say that people buy what they want more often than what they need. Being able to empathise with your reader and convey this in the copy that you write is the key that unlocks the 'know, like and trust' door, which is essential for any transactional relationship.

That empathy needs to extend to the client, as much as to the client's audience. What is it the client needs from the copy you are writing? More sales, better staff retention, a better image? You need to be able to think like the client just as much as understanding their customers.

Collaboration skills

You could argue that collaboration skills are vital in all jobs but that is not necessarily always the case. Translation can be a lonely business, especially for freelance translators who work from home, generally alone and mostly communicate via email. There is little need for collaboration except rarely on large projects, but these are often run by the project manager of a translation agency, and, in my experience, little collaboration work occurs.

The same does not apply to copywriting, however. Most copy is delivered as part of a collaborative project involving graphic designers, web designers, videographers, brand consultants, marketing managers... the list goes on! This will of course depend on the size of the company commissioning the copy, the business owner and the scale of the project. If you are just writing the copy for a blog, for example, you may not need to collaborate with the creative team behind the website as the blog is a stand-alone document that talks about one aspect of your client's business.

However, ensuring brand consistency throughout a copywriting project is crucial to ensure that the copy is fit for purpose and achieves it goals. Unlike in translation, a detailed brief is essential to outline the scope of the work, the tone of voice, the target audience, client avatar, etc. and you will often need to work closely with other people who are involved in the project to achieve the project's aims.

Copywriting is a creative exercise, and working closely with other creatives is not only essential but highly rewarding and leads to better results. After working alone for years in my home office with just my cat for company, I find this part of my copywriting work one of the most enjoyable.

Communication skills

Communication is, of course, key to any relationship, whether it is personal or professional. Not only will you need to communicate with a team of designers and your client, but with your audience. You need to get to know the team you are working with.

If you are a translator, you should have finely-honed communication skills and not be too intimidated by this requirement. If you need to work on this skill, then start communicating more with your current clients via email. Ask them how they are. Find out what they did over the weekend and share a bit about your life.

For years as a translator, I kept my emails formal. I had created generic responses to work requests and return delivery emails. I simply copied and pasted this text into each relevant email. While this saved time, when I look back, I must have sounded like a robot! That all changed when I started learning about copywriting and networking more to promote the copywriting arm of my business.

Injecting personality into your professional persona is a great way to strengthen your relationships with your colleagues and associates. However, just don't overshare - if you had one too many Margaritas over the weekend, that's best kept to yourself!

Project management skills

If you work in the translation industry you may well be a project manager for a translation agency or you may have experience of project management gained from another industry. As a freelance translator, I have found myself juggling multiple projects over the years, often with punishing deadlines that no other industry would tolerate - especially if it had a union behind it - but I managed to do it and continue to do so.

This juggling skill that I involuntarily and passively acquired over the years now stands me in good stead as a copywriter. I can manage projects and deliver on time by carefully assessing milestones and deadlines. The best thing about being a copywriter is that the deadlines are mostly set by me, and I ensure they are realistic and achievable. There are plenty of apps available online that can help you project manage but if it's just you, an Excel sheet should suffice. Whatever system you use, make sure you check it regularly and update it as projects unfold.

An important thing to consider when setting milestones for delivery is to make sure that you have included enough time to edit. No copywriter should ever deliver their first draft or even their second draft. It is essential that when you have written your copy you go away, preferably leaving it at least overnight, and come back and look at it with a fresh pair of eyes. There will always be something you want to tweak. I find the same applies to my translation work. I always leave time between finishing the translation and reviewing it with a fresh pair of eyes before delivery.

Unlike in translation, with copywriting you can determine how much time you need to finish the copy as you are not answerable to a translation agency who has secured the work based on a fast turnaround time. I find this flexibility valuable, as it means that I can take on translation projects with urgent deadlines and still complete my copywriting tasks that have a longer lead time and are less time pressured.

This also helps me during times of feast and famine, which can happen in the translation industry. Often December is exceptionally busy in the translation world with clients wanting everything done by Christmas. So, if I am approached to write copy in December, I will tell my clients that I have a full diary and will schedule it in for January, which tends to be a quiet month, certainly in the first two weeks, for translation.

Of course, the most important aspect of project management is organisation. If you are organised and schedule things correctly you will feel secure in the knowledge that you are controlling the aspects of your business that you do have control over.

Creativity/ideation skills

As I write this it strikes me that these two skills are probably the most important. Without the ability to be original, look at things from a different angle and present things in a fresh, new way, you cannot copywrite successfully.

It's funny when I look back, as my friends growing up were creative, either artistically or musically. I'm a lousy singer and musician and am hopeless at drawing so I never thought I was creative, and neither did my friends, who thought I was odd studying languages.

It was only when I found out my top 5 strengths according to the CliftonStrengths® (https://www.gallup.com/cliftonstrengths/en/home.aspx) that I was able to see that ideation was my number one skill. I wasn't even sure what this meant initially so I looked it up and was thrilled to find out that 'having ideas' can be regarded a skill. Although, as my husband likes to point out, I have loads of ideas, but they're not all good. Luckily, he now filters them for me!

Here's the description provided for ideation in the CliftonStrengths®
Strengthsfinder 2.0:

IDEATION *You are fascinated by ideas. What is an idea? An idea is a concept, the best explanation of most events. You are delighted when you discover beneath the complex surface an elegantly simple concept to explain why things are the way they are. An idea is a connection, and so you are intrigued when seemingly disparate phenomena can be linked by an obscure connection.*

If that description of ideation strikes a chord with you, then you are well suited to copywriting.

Confidence to write boldly

He who dares, wins!

Stepping out of your comfort zone and writing boldly is particularly important for a copywriter. If you can't flip the status quo on its head and disrupt the perception of a product or service, then how will your copy ever stand out from the crowd?

Being bold does not mean making exaggerated claims or writing barefaced lies; it means reading your audience, tapping into the zeitgeist or having an original idea so that your copy can stand out from the competition. This approach takes guts but is worth it. Be prepared to stand up for what you have written and sell it to your client, who may be more conservative in outlook!

Chapter 2
Transferable skills

Plus ça change, plus c'est la même chose
(The more things change, the more they stay the same)

Skills translators and copywriters have in common

At first glance, translating and copywriting might seem like quite different disciplines but, in fact, there are many similarities between the skills you need to do both well. In this chapter, I will describe the skills I have acquired as a translator which I now find particularly useful to draw on in my copywriting.

Six key transferable translating skills

1. Knowing your audience and the purpose of the text
2. Understanding different writing styles
3. Familiarity with the culture/history of the target language country
4. Awareness of recent trends/news events in the target language country
5. Strong writing skills
6. Ability to learn and use new technology

Let's now look at each of these transferable skills to see how they can be transferred to copywriting.

Knowing your audience

As a translator it is useful and important to know the intended reader of the text you are translating. Unfortunately, this information is not always imparted by project managers or direct clients, but it often becomes obvious from the medium being used for the text. For example, a company press release will be read by the public, and particularly by people who are interested in the company or organisation that is releasing it, or it may be used to inform an investment or merger decision or influence someone's decision to apply for a job with a certain company or organisation. By keeping the audience and the purpose of the text in mind at all times the target text will be fit for purpose and hit the right tone with the reader.

An employee handbook, on the other hand, is clearly intended to be read solely by employees and won't be released outside the organisation. This should be reflected in its translation by a more informal, easy-to-read and less journalistic style than a press release.

As a third example, a Patient Information Sheet for a medicinal product (whose target audience is obviously the patient), will be written more in layman's terms than a Summary of Medical Product Characteristics, which will be read by healthcare professionals who need to know how to prescribe the product safely. Of course, a patient may be a medical professional or have an extensive medical vocabulary, but this cannot be assumed. An example of the linguistic differences here would be the use of "liver function" and "kidney function" in the former, and "hepatic function" and "renal function" in the latter.

In copywriting too, it is also vital that you know who your target reader is and the purpose of the copy. If you're writing copy to sell a product or service you need to know who will want to buy it in as much granular detail as possible. This will ensure that the language you use resonates effectively with the client avatar and persuades or convinces them that they need to buy the product or service you are promoting.

Conversely, if you are writing a blog for an aesthetic practitioner who provides Botox and other injectable filler treatments, whose client avatar is a mature, professional female, you need to use the type of language that this demographic would use, as opposed to language that would appeal to a 50-year-old male, for example.

Writing styles

As a translator, you most likely have a degree in at least one language and will have studied different writing styles and be able to identify them. According to a blog on writing styles by Grammarly there are four main writing styles - expository, descriptive, persuasive, and narrative, and they are described as:

Expository writing sets forth facts. You can find it in textbooks, journalism (except opinion or editorial articles), business writing, technical writing, essays, and instructions.

Descriptive writing evokes images through rich description. You can find it in fiction, poetry, journal writing, and advertising.

Persuasive writing aims to sway the reader toward the author's point of view. It is used heavily in advertising and can also be found in opinion and editorial pieces, reviews, and job applications.

Narrative writing tells a story. It can be found in fiction, poetry, biographies, human interest stories, and anecdotes.

Source: https://www.grammarly.com/blog/types-of-writing/

All four writing styles have their place:

- Expository language is used when writing copy for informative articles such as blogs, brochures or longer pieces such as a white paper.
- Copywriters will also often use descriptive writing to paint a picture of what the prospect's life would be like if they purchased the product or service in question. People are more likely to buy a product when the copy is visual, visceral and vivid.

- Copywriters mostly use persuasive writing in website copy, advertising materials and other marketing collateral, to convince leads to make a purchase.
- Narrative or storytelling is a powerful tool for advertising and is frequently deployed to describe to a prospect how someone else with their specific problem benefited from buying the product or service that is for sale.

One example I came across of effective, simple, descriptive and simple copywriting was whilst on holiday in Devon in 2021 when my husband and I visited Dartmouth, home to the Britannia Royal Naval School. There was a sign outside an ice cream booth which was a perfect marriage of copy and graphic design. The board outside an ice cream shop described the ice cream flavours using a descriptive adjective for each flavour such as "zesty lemon" and "velvet chocolate" and the list of flavours was written in the colours of each ice cream flavour; so, chocolate was brown, strawberry was red, etc.

Culture and history of the target language country

As a translator, you will know that it is crucial that you understand the culture of the country of the language you are translating into. This is equally true in copywriting in order for the reader to feel like you are speaking directly to them. This is why it is important to translate and copywrite into your mother tongue and not your second language. There are subtle nuances and key cultural and historical information often only known to natives of a particular country.

A good example of this happened to me in February 2023 when I was translating a financial text from Italian into English and the source text listed various foreign financial sanction lists as below:

U.S. Department of Commerce, la Consolidated List delle Nazioni Unite, la Consolidated List dell'Unione Europea, la

Her Majesty's Treasury Consolidated List o la Foreign Affairs Consolidated List dell'Australia.

Following the passing of Her Majesty, Queen Elizabeth II in September 2022, "*Her* Majesty's Treasury Consolidated List" has been renamed "*His* Majesty's Treasury Consolidated List". Being British, I knew this, but I realised that this was not patently obvious to a non-British audience.

When I delivered my translation, I informed my project manager who worked for a translation agency based in Milan, Italy, in case she was unaware of this convention and the document was being translated into other foreign languages who were also unaware of it. Also, the source text in Italian needed to be amended to reflect this change of name.

In copywriting it is also essential to know the culture of the language you are writing in, to ensure you hit the right tone with the reader and resonate with them fully.

Familiarity with the history of the target language

Knowing the history of the target language country is as important in translation as it is in copywriting, for many of the same reasons as having an in-depth knowledge of the target language culture. As translators, knowing a foreign language means we can access other cultures and thereby become cultural mediators.

A good example of this is provided by the use of "autumn" vs "fall". In British English we use the term autumn, but in the U.S. it is usually referred to as "fall". So, why the discrepancy? The answer stems from our different cultural and linguistic history. After British English was exported to America our official languages and spelling conventions diverged. This is explained below in a quote from Grammarist.

Fall and autumn are both accepted and widely used terms for the season that comes between summer and winter. Some who consider British English the only true English regard fall as an American barbarism, but this attitude is not well founded. Fall is in fact an old term for the season, originating in English in the 16th century or earlier. It was originally short for fall of the year or fall of the leaf, but it commonly took the one-word form by the 17th century, long before the development of American English. So, while the term is now widely used in the U.S., it is not exclusively American, nor is it American in origin."

Source: https://grammarist.com/usage/autumn-fall/

Culture of the target language

Knowing the importance of certain words and where they come from is crucial when creating the desired effect in marketing copy. This approach is also used in political speeches, propaganda and slogans as much as taglines for products. An example of this is the slogan "Keep calm and carry on" which is often seen in Britain on mugs, posters and other merchandise. Its roots lie in a motivational poster used during World War II; the slogan encapsulates the British spirit of resilience and perseverance, and an ability to stay calm in challenging times. It is now an iconic phrase that sums up the tendency of the British people to retain their stiff upper lip and remain composed at all times. It is now viewed as a symbol of British heritage and cultural identity.

When phrases and terms are used often enough, they become part of the identity of a speaker of that language and demonstrate fluency and an understanding of the population that speaks it.

Consider William Tyndale, who translated The Bible into vernacular English for the first time to make it accessible to all and not just the privileged few who could speak Latin and Greek and were mostly clergy. So many of the terms he coined remain with us today and are often used by English speakers. Here are a few examples:

- "And God said, let there be light, and there was light"
- "Fight the good fight"
- "Am I my brother's keeper?"
- "The salt of the earth"
- "The spirit is willing, but the flesh is weak"
- "Eat, drink and be merry"

Source: https://glebereport.ca/articles/william-tyndales-memorable-turns-of-phrase/

Recent trends and news events in the target language country

In translation, understanding the cultural and historical background of a target language country and how it affects the language you use when discussing news events is crucial. If you are translating a financial report, for example, that cites significant events during the financial year in question that have impacted the company's results, you need to tailor your language to fit the target audience. Company annual reports, of which I have translated many, contain a section that reflects on key external events beyond the company's control that have occurred in the previous financial year and that have impacted its financial performance. Recent examples of this include the Covid-19 pandemic and the conflict in Ukraine. Different countries will take a different view on the conflict in Ukraine: countries in NATO view it as a war and yet others, more allied to Russia, will prefer to express it as a 'conflict'. So, it's important to know how the country of the target audience perceives certain events.

The same applies in copywriting; knowing the mood of the country at the time of writing is key to hitting the right note with your target audience and is essential if you want them to persuade people to buy the product or service you are promoting.

For example, at the time of writing this book in 2023, the mood in the UK is one of frugality in the face of a cost-of-living crisis, with stark differences in spending habits and interests between generations. Younger people, commonly referred to as 'Gen Z',[1] are more likely to cancel a subscription such as a gym membership or a streaming service such as Netflix. While Boomers[2] for example are more worried about the situation in Ukraine. Fast fashion is becoming increasingly frowned upon and buying second-hand goods is less stigmatised than before.

Such trends are a reaction to multiple domestic and global events that have severely impacted the British economy, such as Brexit, the Covid-19 pandemic, the war in Ukraine, the cost-of-living crisis and the resulting highest inflation in decades.

All these sentiments need to be weaved into copy so that readers feel understood and that the values of the company they are buying from are aligned with their values. However, be aware of the lifespan of your written piece and ensure you do not include references which make the article appear out of date prematurely.

Strong writing skills

The importance of possessing this skill for a translator or copywriter may seem obvious but the need for the ability to write well in the target language cannot be underestimated. There is a good reason professional translators translate into their mother tongue. We've all read translations that have clearly not been written by a native speaker and lack fluency and flow. This can happen despite the translator having excellent writing skills, yet the level of fluency that is required to write publishable materials can be lost simply by using the wrong preposition: consider "I'm going in Rome" instead of "I'm going to Rome", for example.

Strong writing skills does not just mean knowing the grammar and spelling rules of the target language but being able to manipulate words to prompt a reaction, as in creative language, and weave them together to craft a piece of writing for a specific effect. This is especially useful in copywriting where less is more; using the right word at the right time.

The importance of correct collocations

Another example of excellent writing skills is using correct collocations. According to the Cambridge Dictionary, *"Collocation refers to how words go together or form fixed relationships."*

If there is one thing in Britain we like talking about, it's the weather! There are so many terms with which we describe the British weather, and to do so we use several common collocations. To mix these up and use the incorrect adjective would be immediately noticeable to a native speaker, but not perhaps to someone translating. Some of these are pairings of adjectives + nouns which are just familiar to the British ear; others are expressions which must be in the correct order. Here are some examples:

Typical collocations	*Incorrect/untypical collocations*
Heavy rain and strong winds	~~Strong rain and heavy winds~~
High temperature	~~Big temperature~~
A spell of good weather	~~A period of good weather~~
Raining cats and dogs	~~Raining dogs and cats~~
It will warm up soon	~~It will hot up soon~~

So, although the 'Incorrect/untypical collocations' are not grammatically incorrect and are understandable they lack fluency and are the kinds of mistakes often made by a non-native speaker. A good translator would never say "big temperature" for example, and neither would a good copywriter.

Ability to learn and use new technology

In this fast-paced digital age it is essential that you embrace technology and see it as your friend and not your foe. As a translator, you will undoubtedly have used various CAT (Computer-assisted translation) tools and more recently, machine translation engines powered by AI to speed up your workflow and be as efficient as possible.

When you start copywriting, you will also need to research what tools are available. By tools I am generally referring to applications or software that can help you organise and structure your work and ensure your copy is as engaging as possible. In Chapter 11 I explore the whole world of copywriting and AI, a fast-changing scenario which you need to be aware of. It's important to find out what tools your competitors are using and the benefits of using such tools to save time and improve the quality of your work.

COPY THAT!

Chapter 3
Overcoming your fears

"The only thing we have to fear is fear itself."
Franklin D. Roosevelt

Starting with a blank page

How to overcome the fear of starting with a blank page

When I started copywriting back in 2019, I had been a full-time freelance translator for twelve years, which meant I had been translating a plethora of documents from a variety of industries for a wide range of target audiences. I was confident about my understanding of my three source languages (Italian, French and Spanish) and my ability to render a well-written translation into English (my target language) that read as though it had been written in English original. If it didn't, I hadn't done my job properly.

However, the one thing I hadn't done in all those years was write new text from scratch. To do so successfully now required a whole additional set of skills and considerations:

- Defining the purpose of the text
- Defining the target audience
- Organising the structure of the document
- Collating ideas
- Considering the sequence of the text and drawing conclusions
- Factoring in how the reader FEELS
- Structuring the features/benefits of the product or service I am trying to promote, using AIDA[3] proficiently
- And formulating a clear call to action

That is quite a list of additional tasks! I will be covering these in detail in Chapter 7 in Part 3, but for now this list is a recognition of the shift in thinking which is needed when starting with that blank page.

As a result of my years of translating texts written by someone else in another language, I hadn't consciously realised that I hadn't written anything myself for years, other than emails and social media posts. So, as you can imagine, the first thing I did on my first copywriting assignment was break out in a cold sweat! I'm telling you this because, if you are a translator, it may well happen to you, depending on how much you have written professionally, for yourself or for clients, outside of a translating context in recent years.

Strategies to overcome your fear

Like any well-executed task, it's all about the planning. In translation, for me there was a feeling of safety derived from the fact that someone else had written the document; I just had to translate it for the target audience. In this case, the planning came from studying any glossaries that the client provided, reading the text in full, identifying the key terminology, and researching the best translation for each term, depending on the type of text I was translating.

I always remember one of the lecturers on my Master's in translation course telling us that terminology is, on average, 20% of any document, so it's a bit like cracking a code - once you've identified the key terms, the rest falls into place.

Consider, for example, the words "*azioni*" and "*esercizio*" in Italian. In most translations into English, they would be translated respectively as "actions" and "exercise". In a financial text, however, they have a quite different meaning and are, in fact, faux amis (false friends) i.e. words that seem to have a similar meaning in two languages but can actually have a completely different meaning. "*Azioni*" refers to shares/stock and "*esercizio*" is the financial year or accounting period in question.

A non-specialist in this field would not be aware of this and would deliver a translation of an Annual Report that would have references to 'actions' and 'exercises', but no mention of shares or the financial year the figures refer to thus rendering it at best meaningless and at worst nonsensical to a potential investor or shareholder in the company interested in finding out about its performance.

In copywriting, the best strategy for overcoming any fear of starting with a blank page is to conduct some research, which immediately creates some safe ground from which to gain in confidence. This could be competitor research, or identifying your client avatar and studying how that demographic speaks and what is important to them in terms of values and world view.

Once you feel you have researched your subject sufficiently, then comes the planning of the document. Here it is important to consider the features/benefits of the product or service and how best to implement AIDA. Only when you have a clear roadmap and structure for the copy you want to write will you be able to get started, free of fear and confident that you know exactly what you want to say, how you are going to say it and the order in which you are going to present it.

So, what was my first copywriting assignment? My first ever copywriting client was a Brazilian cakemaker from Brighton who needed a copywriter to write the About page for her website, as English wasn't her first language. I knew her quite well and how talented she was, as she had made a beautiful handmade football-themed cake for my dad's 70th birthday party, which he loved. Having been a customer made it easy for me to write her About page as I understood how passionate she was about her work.

As a non-native speaker of English, this cakemaker wanted it to sound natural to an English-speaking audience and to resonate with her target audience, which were local artisan bakeries, coffee shops, beauty salons and people wanting a bespoke birthday for a cherished loved one. Once we had discussed the above it became clear to me that although she was a fantastic cakemaker, her USP was her love of colour and a flamboyancy that stemmed from her Brazilian heritage and traditions.

Here's the first piece of copy I ever wrote, for this About page, anonymised here at the request of my Brazilian friend:

A came over to the UK from Brazil in 1998. Since then, her family has grown and she now has had two beautiful daughters who she has always loved baking for. This is where her passion for cakes sprang from. When her daughters were small, she would fill the house with the aroma of freshly baked bread that she baked herself for the family. This passion for baking then developed into a desire to bake cakes and sweet pastries.

A's Brazilian heritage and culture played a big part in her wanting to express herself in colours and forms and generally brighten up the all too frequent dark, damp English days. She was able to do this by designing and making beautiful cakes. A soon discovered that baking cakes was something she had a natural talent for and which she found was immensely rewarding; not only that, it provided a great excuse to invite people over and entertain. Through her love of baking and flair for design, not to mention her warm, Latin personality she made lots of new friends and was able to bring some Brazilian colour and flair to those around her and bridge cultural divides that sometimes words alone cannot.

Driven by her passion to bake and create, A set up a business over ten years ago to put her finely-honed skills to practical use. Since then, she has never had a cake suggestion she has been unable to fulfil, from a replica guitar and amp for a musician, to unicorns and a beer keg shaped cake; she can literally cater for all tastes. A loves a challenge and relishes new requests that test her skills as an artisan; she now boasts an eclectic back catalogue of unique and delicious cakes. See some of A's work on her gallery page – you won't be disappointed!

A prides herself on being an artisan confectioner and cake maker and now works with corporate clients providing them with cakes that reflect their brand and impress their customers and colleagues, whether they are a hotel, a lawyer's firm or a beauty salon, she meets their needs by offering exquisite, freshly baked cakes and sweet pastries to order and takes the stress out of sourcing one-off, bespoke, scrumptious cakes.

When I look back at this now, of course there are things that I would change, but what got me over the fear of starting with a blank page was talking to A and getting her to tell me in her own words why she started making bespoke cakes and what she enjoys about it.

I wanted to tell her story to the world and convey the passion she has for cakemaking on a deep, personal level and how it connects her with home and family. I felt sure that once people read about her passion for her work, they would want to sample her cakes.

Three years and many cakes later, A's business is thriving, which isn't surprising because her cakes are absolutely delicious!

So, who do you know that needs copywriting services? A beautician, car mechanic or plumber perhaps. If you think about it hard enough, you will think of someone who would appreciate your written skills applied to their marketing materials.

If you can't think of anyone, study the marketing materials that come through your door or in your local newspaper and look for someone who has clearly written the copy themselves and you believe you can improve it. Contact them and explain that you are a copywriter and have a special offer on or explain how you could improve their copy so that it is more impactful.

Failing that, look at your own business. Decide on a specific service that you want to promote. Write a blog, landing page or article about it or offer to do the same for a friend, family member or colleague. The more you write the more your confidence will grow, and a blank page will become something you look forward to instead of something you fear.

Chapter 4
Owning it!

"*Carthago delenda est*"
[*Carthage must be destroyed*]
Cato

Reinventing yourself and believing it

One of the hardest things when you pivot your career in another direction is fighting the urge to succumb to that popular but overused phrase 'imposter syndrome'. If you have been a translator for several years, as I had when I started copywriting, it felt odd and unnatural to suddenly show up and call myself a copywriter. One thing I learned early on was that if you don't believe it, no-one else will!

Say it and it will happen!

In Ancient Rome, Cato, a Roman Senator, was known to repeat the phrase *"Carthago delenda est"* ["Carthage must be destroyed"] three times after every speech during debates held in the Senate prior to the Third Punic War (149–146 BC). Eventually, Carthage was destroyed.

I applied this philosophy to launching as a copywriter. In the autumn of 2019, I attended a marketing course for translators at the head office of the ITI (Institute for Translation and Interpreting), in which we were advised to write up our LinkedIn profiles from the perspective of how we want to be perceived and what we want to become. The idea being 'say it and it will be true'.

I took this advice, and it has worked really well, not only in terms of boosting my confidence, but also in creating an accurate perception of how I want other people to see me.

The belief that you are now a copywriter must start with you. Just as you might update your LinkedIn profile, website or online persona to reflect new skills that you have learned, now it's time to add 'copywriter' to your services.

So, this idea of saying it and it will be true can be applied to pivoting your business or adding an additional service. There is huge value not only in saying things aloud, as in the case of Cato, but in writing them down.

Once you have decided you are ready to launch as should any copywriter, make sure that your LinkedIn profile reflects this, as does any other business social media accounts you may have. If you're on TikTok or an equivalent platform, talk about it in your videos. Create a landing page on your website for your new service and add a section to your Home page that mentions it.

By writing it into your marketing materials you will start to believe it and feel the pressure of needing to deliver, which you need in the beginning to get your adrenalin going. This will help you to generate the great copy you know you are capable of!

Complete a copywriting course

Another way to boost your confidence and feel more credible when you go to market is to complete a course on copywriting. I did this and it really helped me to realise that copywriting is a different writing skill to translation. However, the good news is that once I understood the main principles behind writing to sell or educate and inform, I could draw on my extensive knowledge of language gained through my translation work. I could then just focus on the empathy side of my writing: understanding and describing features and benefits; being clear on problems solved; and why someone would want to buy the product or service.

Another benefit of completing a copywriting course is that, if you pick the right course, it will offer opportunities to practise what you have learned, which will further boost your confidence levels.

There are so many e-learning courses available now online that it is worth researching the best one for you in terms of time, cost and value. A good way of finding the best course for you is to read testimonials to find out if they were satisfied and if their needs are aligned with yours.

What to look for in a copywriting course

The type of course which worked for me:

- A gradual step-by-step approach
- An online course that I could complete at my own pace
- Practical exercises to complete

The aspects of course content I found most helpful:

- Tried and tested marketing strategies
- The art of persuasion
- How to influence buying decisions
- Learning about AIDA and how to apply it

Face-to-face networking

If you haven't done much face-to-face networking outside of your industry, and if you want to launch a new career as a copywriter, you will need to start to find clients and learn how to pitch your business.

This form of networking can be quite daunting, but it is a great way to find clients. Most formal networking groups either meet once a week or once a month and require members to deliver a 60-second pitch. This is where you will really grow in confidence and can showcase your writing skills.

In January 2020, I joined a face-to-face weekly networking group and found it terrifying but exhilarating initially. Of course, in March 2020, the group went online during the various lockdowns due to Covid-19 and then back to in-person meetings.

I now attend a variety of networking meetings, from a weekly structured online group to in-the-room open networking where there are no pitches.

Networking is a long game and is all about relationship building. It is unlikely that anyone will buy from you at the first meeting as it takes time to build strong relationships. People tend to buy from you when they know, like and trust you. One of the key skills a copywriter needs is empathy - being in tune with a client's objectives and needs. That empathy can best be achieved by getting to know, like and trust each other through networking. You can read more about networking in Part Five.

Hire a coach or mentor

I found working with a business coach helped me tremendously, as he provided unbiased support and advice. He also helped me to dispel any false and self-limiting beliefs that crept into my mind and got in the way of me moving my business forward. If you need impartial encouragement and someone who will hold you accountable, hiring a business coach is one of the best ways to do it and should be viewed as an investment and not a cost.

Ignore the naysayers

My journey into translation was not straightforward and may reflect some of the ups and downs you may go through when changing or adapting your career. Between 2004 and 2006 I was a French and Spanish teacher in a secondary school in West Sussex. When I entered the teaching profession my children were both at primary school, so I thought it would be perfect as we would keep the same hours and I would be free to look after them in the school holidays. That was not the case, however, as I worked in a different school in a different town and was dependent on childcare to get them to school and pick them up and look after them if they were sick.

Initially, my mum did this for me but unfortunately her health took a turn for the worse and I needed to find an alternative solution. I left teaching to do a Master's in Translation so that I could work from home and wouldn't have to be reliant on anyone else to look after my children.

When I told my fellow teachers that I was leaving teaching they were shocked, especially the ones who had been there for decades and were on the brink of retirement. "What about your pension?" they cried and "Watch out, translation is a very unreliable industry". Although I took their comments onboard and started to doubt my decision to leave, I stuck to my guns, followed my gut and went for it. I'm proud to say that I graduated in 2007 with a distinction and launched my translation career in 2007. Despite the naysayers, ten years later I had quadrupled my income. I urge you to do the same if it feels right for you.

> *"Do something today that your future self will thank you for."*
>
> *Sean Patrick Flannery*

Tasks to complete

1. Create or edit your LinkedIn profile so it represents who you want to be in 12 months' time

2. Try out some networking groups, ideally in your industry and in other industries that might need your services

3. Write a blog post or landing page for a service you provide

4. Ask a friend/colleague if you can write some copy for them

5. Start looking out for and listening to ads

6. When you buy something online ask yourself what made you buy it. Look at marketing emails differently. Do they hook you in with the subject line and make you want to open them? What's in the subject line? Why did you open it? Did you buy from it?

7. Keep up to date with UK trends or target language trends, buzzwords and social values

COPY THAT!

Part two

COPY THAT!

Chapter 5
Getting started

"You don't have to be great to start, but you have to start to be great."
Zig Ziglar

Passive steps

Where to begin?

As with any new endeavour, getting in the mindset of someone who does what you want to become is important. So, if you want to become a copywriter, you must think like a copywriter. How do you start to think like a copywriter? The best way is to start listening to copywriters via your preferred medium or media.

In Chapter 4 we discussed the value of completing a course on copywriting. This is one way to familiarise yourself with the practice of copywriting, but unless you have a tutor who is very generous with their time, you are unlikely to gain access to their day-to-day struggles or understand what pitfalls you need to avoid. Furthermore, a course will not teach you what it's like writing for different industries, client types and the daily aspects of being a copywriter.

The value of podcasts

For me, one of the best ways of overcoming this was by listening to podcasts by copywriters and marketers. I found this a valuable source of knowledge about what it is like being a copywriter and what problems copywriters face: how they deal with clients, how much they charge, how they respond to customer feedback, etc. I also follow copywriters on LinkedIn, my preferred social media platform. Doing this gives me insights into other people's businesses and how they approach copywriting.

One of my favourite podcasts is *Copywriters Podcast*, https://copywriterspodcast.com which features David Garfinkel, a well-established and respected American copywriter and copy coach. The podcast drops a new episode weekly and discusses various topics around copywriting.

One of the most insightful episodes is episode no. 156. It forms part of the podcast's 'Old Masters Series', and it discusses a book, first published in 1916 as a short story in an American newspaper, called *Obvious Adams*[4]. The easiest way to access this is via YouTube. Enter 'Obvious Adams, Old Masters Series—Copywriters Podcast 156' in YouTube search to find it.

The book is by Robert R. Updegraff and is subtitled, 'The Story of a Successful Businessman'. What the book teaches us is the enduring value of writing with clarity. Updegraff uses the art of storytelling to explain the importance of knowing your audience. The premise of the story is that after visiting a paper mill looking to hire an ad agency to advertise its products, the main character, Obvious Adams, spends two days learning the intricacies of how paper is manufactured. He then comes back to the client with his proposal, which describes how paper is made in explicit detail: *"Every good bond paper is made with pure filtered water; every good bond paper is loft-dried; all good papers are hand inspected."*

The client responds that he would be *"the laughing stock of all the paper makers in the country if they saw us come out and talk that way about our paper when all of the good ones make their paper that way."* To which Adams replies, *"Mr. Merritt, to whom are you advertising – paper makers or paper users?"*

Despite the age of the book, the message it conveys remains the same: understand who your true audience is and communicate clearly, even if that seems 'Obvious Adams' to the client:

- Write from the viewpoint of the product's/service's users, not your client
- What may be obvious to you and the client is not necessarily obvious to their customers

- Quality is often best conveyed by describing processes and procedures
- Don't be afraid to go into detail - if people have a small level of interest in something you can build on that with 'insider' industry info
- Looking at the brief quotation above, consider the power of the two-word phrase 'loft-dried'. It evokes so many connotations: artisanship, care, time spent, optimum manufacturing conditions, heritage, knowledge and experience. All terms which make you feel that this is a quality paper worth paying a premium for.

Use 5 tests

A few years after it was first published, the author added the '5 Tests of Obviousness', which are listed below:

1. The problem, when solved, will be simple
2. Does it check with human nature?
3. Put it on paper
4. Does it explode in people's minds?
5. Is the time ripe?

So, as an example, how can we apply these tests to a well-known and highly effective marketing campaign? The example they give in the podcast is Apple's famous tagline used to launch its revolutionary iPod in October 2001. The ad and its tagline were wonderfully simple: on the left a picture of an iPod, with its revolutionary pinwheel navigation below its screen. On the right, just this text:

iPod.
1,000 Songs in your pocket.

Test 1 - The problem, when solved, will be simple

Imagine the technology, maths and creativity that went into designing the iPod! At the time, there were other MP3 players on the market, but these could only store about 100 songs and were way behind in the intuitive, sleek design department. 1,000 songs, a little mad though it seems now, was a stunning amount of choice to carry in your pocket!

Every product exists to solve a problem. In this case, the problem was storing a library of your favourite songs in a light, "ultra-portable" device (as described by Steve Jobs in his keynote launch speech delivered on 23 October 2001), but what's clever about the copy here is that it goes straight to the heart of what a buyer wants to hear: a simple solution to their portable music library problem.

Does it pass the test? YES!

Test 2 - Does it check with human nature?

This means, can you explain it to a five-year-old, your partner, your grandmother, your hairdresser, or anyone else you know, and crucially, will they get it?

"1,000 songs in your pocket" is understandable by anyone of any age or generation.

Does it pass the test? YES!

Test 3 - Put it on paper

Here the test is to write it down and see how it looks. Does it contain words of 1 or 2 syllables? Yes, there are no long or complicated industry-specific words in the tagline, so it reads clearly on the page.

Does it pass the test? YES!

Test 4 - Does it explode in people's minds?
You bet it does! Back in 2001, the iPod was at the cutting – no, scrap that - bleeding edge of user-friendly tech, and no other product on the market looked or performed as well as the iPod. It literally blew everyone's mind. Its revolutionary navigation style of turning a touch-wheel to find a song was such a stylish and clever solution to finding a song quickly. Not only does the tagline conjure up an image, but it's also tangible. You can imagine holding the device in your hand and then slipping it in your pocket.

Does it pass the test? YES!

Test 5 - Is the time ripe?
This one is slightly tricky, as the iPod launched soon after the 9/11 attack on the World Trade Center in New York, so these were unsettling times, especially in the U.S.

However, the iPod's success is a testament to the fact that the world *was* ready for this device, which ultimately paved the way for the smartphones we all carry around with us everywhere today.

Does it pass the test? YES!

The value of podcasts

The reason for sharing this story is to demonstrate how much value a podcast can offer by sharing knowledge, past and present, gained over many years by experts in the field. Had I not listened to this podcast it would have taken longer to stumble across the book *Obvious Adams* and discover the '5 Tests of Obviousness' and how they provided a clear example of how the tests can be applied to the Apple iPod. Boy, I wish I had listened to this episode right at the start of my copywriting journey!

So, whether you are currently a translator or not, and you want to start copywriting, my advice is to start by inhabiting the world of other copywriters and learning from them.

Genres of books to read

If you are an expert in marketing or a marketing translator, you may already have a good understanding of the approach you need to take when copywriting. However, if this is not the case, I recommend not only reading books related to copywriting, but also to advertising, marketing, and even psychology.

The reason for this is simple. If you plan on writing copy to sell or persuade, you will need to understand people's motivation for buying and what they respond to. I advise reading marketing and advertising books by well-known authors and leaders in the field, even if they wrote their books decades ago, such as Eugene Schwartz, Joe Sugarman, John Caples, Victor O. Schwab and David Ogilvy. Why? Simply because people don't change. Only the technology that is used to deliver the messaging changes.

There are examples of graffiti in Pompeii and Herculaneum dating back to the Roman times advertising gladiatorial games; so, copywriting is not a new phenomenon. The media we use to publish and display it has evolved, that's all.

The purpose of this book is not to tell you which books you should read, which will depend on your knowledge and skills, but guide you in your choice of genres. I have included a non-definitive list at the end of this book called Recommended Reading, as a way for me to share the books that I have found valuable and set you down the path to discovering more about your new industry.

Start to consume adverts differently

Whether you realise it or not, by deciding to become a copywriter, you are about to enter the advertising industry. After having spent a lifetime being on the receiving end of adverts on television, the radio, the internet and when walking down the street reading billboards, you now need to consume them differently.

What do I mean by this? I mean read, watch and listen to them and try to determine their effectiveness. Are they any good? Do they make you want to buy? Can you tell by the language used who their target audience is? For example, an advert for a luxury car is not going to be aimed at lower-income people. An advert for an energy drink is probably going to be aimed at a younger audience, etc. Does the ad explain simply what problem it solves and for whom? How does it do that?

Once you start doing this, you won't be able to stop. You will look at every marketing email in your inbox differently, and you will start to ask yourself, "Is that a good subject line?", "Does it make me want to open the email?" And then, when you do open a marketing email, ask yourself, "What made me open that email?" Once you have read the email or ad, ask yourself what you were drawn to. Did it offer a solution to a problem that you have?

When you open an email because of an appealing subject line, think, wow, that worked, it made me open it, but why? Emails that you subscribe to from your favourite brands are a great place to start because you *are* their target audience. The copy in their subject lines should make you want to open them, and the text in the body of the email should make you want to buy.

Analysing what works and what doesn't in adverts is so easy because we are constantly bombarded with advertising every day, and the marketing we receive is increasingly targeting us based on our gender, tastes and preferences.

I recommend also looking and listening out for adverts that aren't targeted at you, when you are out and about, listening to the radio, or just walking down the street or on public transport. Play a game in your mind by answering the following questions:

- Who is that advert targeting?
- What problem is that product or service solving?
- If I had that problem, would I want to buy that product or service to solve it, based on the advert?

By doing this regularly, you can use your time effectively by researching your new profession while out with friends, listening to the radio while driving or watching your favourite TV show. If you are a translator, do this when visiting a country where you speak the language; ask why an advert works for that specific country and culture.

What's your favourite advert of all time?

In my experience, everyone has an advert they remember and recall fondly. This may be one from their childhood, for their favourite food or just because the advert affected them for some reason.

One of my favourite examples from a copywriting perspective is Heinz's 'Beanz Meanz Heinz' baked beans campaign. This simple 3-word slogan using the "z" from Heinz at the end of 'Beanz' and 'Meanz' is simply genius.

Heinz made their brand famous off the back of this campaign, and in the UK, Heinz baked beans are still the best brand of beans money can buy, which is reflected in their premium price. Considering this slogan was first released in 1967, that is over 50 years of ROI (return on investment), not bad for three little words, eh?

So, how did Heinz achieve this phenomenal success? By appealing to their target audience in 1967, which was housewives who wanted to feed their families the best beans possible. At the time, most women were homemakers and managed the food budget while trying to give their children the most nutritious meal possible. Heinz set themselves apart by suggesting that their beans were the only beans you should choose, and all other brands were inferior, without saying so explicitly. It's very clever copywriting.

What's your favourite advertising slogan of all time? Start to think about this and ask yourself what you like about it and why it works for the brand and the audience.

Active steps

Write your own strapline

In 2019, when I decided to become a copywriter, I was running a limited company called AMG Translations Limited. I then created a separate company called ARC Copywriting, and one of the first things I did when I decided to be a copywriter was to write my own strapline, which was 'Because good copy matters'.

For the first year and a half of marketing myself as a copywriter, I would use this strapline at the end of a pitch and in my marketing materials. People would say it back to me in the end, so it clearly resonated.

In 2021, however, after the pandemic hit and everything went online, as a member of BNI (Business Networking International) I found myself visiting groups in Europe and Canada with a virtual Zoom background that said ARC Copywriting. So, now I was reaching an international audience and so I wanted to talk about translation as well as copywriting. I decided to merge my translation business and my copywriting services under one umbrella company so that my messaging was clear. After all, I couldn't tell my clients that their messaging was wrong if mine was.

For reasons of clarity, I called my new business ARC Writing and Translation Services, and created a new strapline, which I still use, which is 'Helping you get your message across'. For me, this new strapline conveyed what I do in both arms of my business. In my translation work, I provide a service to companies which need to be understood culturally and linguistically in a different market or country. In copywriting, I also help my clients to communicate clearly to their target audience what they do and how they can help them overcome a particular problem.

How to write a good strapline

If you are a translator who wants to add copywriting to your portfolio of services, then I suggest you write a strapline that describes what you do. In my opinion, it is a good idea to research other straplines from a range of industries and decide which ones you like best and then ask yourself why you like them. Try to be as clear as possible about what you do and explain the problem you solve and for whom, and most importantly, try to make it memorable and repeatable.

For example, if you are a legal translator, think about how you can express that in 3 or 4 words that target your clients' pain points. Try to think of how you will market yourself as a copywriter. What will distinguish you from your competitors? What message do you want to get across? It's not as easy as it sounds, but, as Obvious Adams would say, "The problem, when solved, will be simple".

You will likely find yourself writing a few at first until you find one that works best. I suggest asking your friends, family or colleagues what they think of your strapline and which one they prefer. Running your strapline through the '5 Tests of Obviousness' is also a good idea.

If you already have a strapline you're happy with, offer to write a strapline for a friend or colleague who doesn't have one. Or take a company of your choice, real or imagined, and create a strapline that works for them.

Work on your storytelling

Once upon a time, a translator decided to become a copywriter…

One thing you will need to do when you are a copywriter that you won't have been required to do in your translation work is tell stories in a way that connects with people (unless you are one of the approx. 5% of translators who specialises in translating literature or are a fiction writer). I suggest you start by listening to other people's stories. Who do you know that is a brilliant storyteller? What makes their stories so engaging and memorable? Do they paint a picture in your mind using vivid language? Is there a clear hero and a villain? Is there an obstacle that needs to be overcome to achieve a goal? Is there a clear structure to the story, i.e., a beginning, middle and end?

Conversely, who do you know who is bad at telling stories? Ask yourself why their stories are so bad. Do they lack focus? Are you not invested in the characters as a listener? Does the narrator take too long to get to the point? Is there a point to the story? Is there no clear lesson that can be learnt from the story?

By examining the stories you hear every day from friends, colleagues and families, you will start to identify what makes a good story and what doesn't. You can also start examining TV shows and films and consider how they tell the story. You can then apply this to the stories you tell when recounting an event that happened to you or to your friend, partner or associates. At the end of the story, ask your audience what the story made them feel. Good stories evoke emotion in the listener; bad stories fail to make the listener feel anything. The same applies to copywriting, so underestimate the value of storytelling at your peril.

Once you have fine-tuned your own storytelling abilities, you will find it easier to use storytelling later on in your copywriting, as you will then be a well-practised storyteller and have an innate, almost subconscious idea of what the essential ingredients for a good story are.

A good book to help guide when you start storytelling for business is *Building a StoryBrand* by Donald Miller.[5] Here's an extract from the book's description on Amazon:

> *"The StoryBrand process is a proven solution to the struggle business leaders face when talking about their companies. Without a clear, distinct message, customers will not understand what you can do for them and are unwilling to engage, causing you to lose potential sales, opportunities for customer engagement, and much more.*
>
> *In Building a StoryBrand, Donald Miller teaches marketers and business owners to use the seven universal elements of powerful stories to dramatically improve how they connect with customers and grow their businesses."*
>
> *So, now you have a clear idea of how to get started, take the first steps to your new career as a professional copywriter.*

Tasks to complete

1. Start listening to podcasts about copywriting

2. Read or listen to books about copywriting, marketing, the psychology of buying and advertising

3. Consume ads differently

4. Write your own strapline

5. Listen to how others tell stories

6. Work on your storytelling abilities by writing short stories

Part three

COPY THAT!

Chapter 6
The art and science of copywriting

"*Copy is not written. Copy is assembled.*"
Eugene Schwartz

This section of the book is devoted to providing you with a toolkit that you can use to leverage your existing skills as a wordsmith in the capacity of a translator and refocus them for a copywriting context. It is broken down into manageable chunks that address the fundamental pillars of effective messaging via the medium of copywriting.

Know your audience

It sounds simple enough, but to craft copy that works, it is vital that you ask yourself the following questions before you write anything:

1. Who are you talking to?
2. What is the purpose of the copy?
3. What tone of voice should you use?
4. What do you want the reader to do after reading the copy?
5. What language does your reader use?

As a translator, you will be familiar with considering the target audience, but you must drill down to a much more detailed level in copywriting.

Firstly, let's consider an occasion in translation when you must be aware of your audience and translate accordingly. A clear example in my translation work as a pharmaceutical translator is knowing the difference between the audience for an SmPC (Summary of medical Product Characteristics) and a package leaflet.

In the first case, an SmPc is written for healthcare professionals familiar with medical terminology. So, for example, you would translate the French term "insuffisance hépatique" as "hepatic impairment". In the second case, however, a package leaflet is intended for the medicinal product user with no assumed medical knowledge. Therefore, you would translate the same term as "liver failure".

Other examples outside the pharmaceutical field include the different writing styles you would adopt for a press release compared to a company's Code of Ethics. In the first case, you need to use engaging, positive language that promotes and informs about a new initiative or development at the company to an external audience. In contrast, the second example requires using values-based language because you are writing about the company's expectations regarding conduct, values and beliefs. In this case, the readership will include employees and external stakeholders such as possible investors.

Let's look at how we identify whom we're talking to in copywriting, using the five points listed above.

Who are you talking to?

Working out precisely to whom the copy is talking takes time and is a process that should not be rushed. Your client may already have determined who their client avatar, also known as buyer/client persona, is, and be able to tell you exactly who they are, what age they are, what their interests are, what their values are, etc., but often, clients do not know themselves. They will think of their ideal client in broad terms or as "anyone really".

An example is an estate agent who might claim, "It's anyone over 18 who wants to buy or sell a house". Or a garden centre team might say, "It's anyone with a garden who wants a shed or plants". While this may be true on the surface, you can help them to focus in on their ideal client by asking them a series of questions. These should be answered based on their dream client or one of their best clients.

Once the business owner can see the value of attracting more of their dream clients, they will be more open to the idea of you writing the copy to appeal to that focused audience by tailoring your messaging to match the specific needs of their client avatar.

Determining a client avatar

To build up a picture of your client's client avatar, you must deploy your research skills, which should already be finely honed as a translator. Start with the data your client already has: analytics from their website, customer satisfaction surveys, social media insights or other data which shows who buys their products and/or services.

This data enables you to start to create a detailed profile of their client avatar. You then need to ask your client a series of questions to determine who they perceive to be their ideal client for each relevant product or service.

For example, a company selling gym equipment will target people for whom keeping fit is essential and who live an active life. Depending on the equipment they specialise in, they will then narrow this down to people of a particular age group with a similar level of income and lifestyle and value choices.

The questions you ask must focus on determining the avatar's age, gender identity, occupation, location, values, interests, personal and professional challenges, goals, aspirations and geographical location. It's also essential to get the messaging right in the copy so you need to determine some psychographic information about the avatar. A wide range of tools and templates are available online to help you create a set of questions that identify your ideal client.

Gathering psychographic information

Psychographic information is a term used to describe the psychological and behavioural characteristics of an individual or a group of people. It means understanding your avatar's values, interests, attitudes, lifestyle choices, motivations, opinions and aspirations. Examining this information will give you a deeper insight into the buying behaviours, preferences, personality traits and decision-making processes the client avatar is prone to.

Psychographic information typically includes:

- Interests, hobbies, passions and recreational pursuits
- Lifestyle choices: habits, routines, and work, leisure, travel and consumption preferences
- Personality traits: are they more introverted or extroverted, adventurous or cautious, spontaneous or routine-led?
- Values and beliefs: what social, environmental or ethical issues matter to them?
- Attitudes and opinions: what are their views on specific brands or products?

Once you have gathered all the information you need, you should ask the client to ascribe a name to their avatar, to give it even more of a focused persona. Go online and find a stock image you can use to attach to the client avatar's profile. This will help you feel like you are addressing an actual person when you are writing the copy. This prior research will enable you to adopt a conversational style in written form that will appeal to and resonate with the client avatar you have established by being aligned with their interests, values and aspirations.

Outline your buyer persona's typical day

To help breathe life into your client avatar, map out their typical day so that you have a deeper understanding of what makes them tick daily, their priorities, and how they manifest in their daily life.

Here is an example of this:

"During the week, John gets up at 7 o'clock, hops in the shower, gets dressed and takes the dog for a walk. Then he returns, eats a healthy breakfast, checks his email and dresses for work. He works in the office two days a week, and the other three days he works from home. On the days he works from home, he walks around the local town at lunchtime and listens to audiobooks about business development. After work, he likes to go to the gym, then comes home and cooks a nutritious meal that he eats with his girlfriend before watching a drama series on TV, and then he goes to bed at 11 pm."

This short but succinct description of John's typical day shows that he likes to follow a routine. He is in a relationship that matters to him. He likes dogs and enjoys keeping fit and eating healthily. We also know that he wants to relax with his girlfriend in front of the TV at the end of the day and goes to bed at a reasonable time.

Copy strategy: identifying the purpose of the copy

All copy needs a strategy, and this should be determined by discussing with the client why they need the copy and what they want it to achieve. The best way to do this is by asking your client the following questions before you start writing and preparing your brief and quote. A clear copy strategy will identify if you need to factor in more time to spend researching industry trends or what your client's competitors are doing to write copy that is aligned with your client's expectations and wishes.

There are several different reasons for writing copy. They can vary, from selling a product or service to demonstrating authority in a given field, entertaining, educating, informing, etc. Knowing the purpose of the copy you have been hired to write is essential. If the purpose is unclear to you, make sure you ask the client what they want the copy to do.

Questions to ask your client:

1. Why do you need this copy?
2. What area of your business are you trying to improve with this copy?
3. What do you want your audience to do after they read the copy?
4. What are you trying to achieve overall with the copy? (E.g., attract new customers, build an online audience, generate new leads, drive conversions or educate your audience about your products/services)

Let's consider putting together the brief for a blog post. There can be several different purposes for a blog post: demonstrating expertise, providing tips and tricks, answering frequently asked questions, and many others besides. To write the best blog for your client, it is vital that you ask what they want the blog to achieve. If they are unsure, discuss it with them further by asking questions such as:

- "Do you want to show your expertise in this area?"
- "Do you want to help your reader to achieve something with tips and tricks?"
- "Do you want to provide answers to frequently asked questions?"

Tone of voice

As a translator, you may be more familiar with talking about the 'register' than a text's 'tone of voice', as this falls more under marketing terminology. At some point, you may have received style guides from a client to be adhered to in your translation. In marketing, however, the tone of voice must be established *before* writing any copy, and it is imperative for brand consistency that this is used throughout the client's marketing collateral, from their website to marketing emails and everything in between.

Larger clients who have worked with a branding company will often have already determined their tone of voice, and it will be written in their brand guidelines. Brand guidelines primarily focus on a brand's visual identity but will also specify the tone of voice. On the other hand, smaller clients will need guidance and help on this to establish their brand's tone of voice.

What is 'tone of voice'?

In simple terms, the tone of voice you are writing in on your client's behalf should reflect the style of interaction they wish to have with their customers. When I start working with a new client who has never considered their tone of voice and doesn't have any brand guidelines in place, I help them to identify the correct tone of voice by asking them to highlight approx. 6-8 of the following tone of voice descriptors that best reflect how they want to come across to their clients.

List of detailed tone descriptors

1.	Authoritative	16.	Funny
2.	Caring	17.	Humorous
3.	Cheerful	18.	Informative
4.	Coarse	19.	Irreverent
5.	Conservative	20.	Matter of fact
6.	Conversational	21.	Nostalgic
7.	Casual	22.	Passionate
8.	Dry	23.	Playful
9.	Edgy	24.	Professional
10.	Engaging	25.	Provocative
11.	Enthusiastic	26.	Quirky
12.	Formal	27.	Respectful
13.	Frank	28.	Romantic
14.	Friendly	29.	Sarcastic
15.	Fun	30.	Serious

31.	Smart		*35.*	Trustworthy
32.	Snarky		*36.*	Unapologetic
33.	Sympathetic		*37.*	Upbeat
34.	Trendy		*38.*	Witty

Source: https://www.nngroup.com/articles/tone-voice-words/

What do you want the reader to do after reading the copy?

This part relates to the action or outcome your copy should achieve. When writing any copy, you need to focus throughout the process on what you want the reader to do once they have read it.

In some cases, this may be obvious. For example, if you're writing sales copy, you will want the reader to be prompted to make a purchase. If you're writing an informative piece to showcase your client's knowledge and expertise, you may just want to build authority and trust. So, instead of pushing for a sale, you now just want the reader to subscribe to a newsletter or follow the client on social media.

Whatever action you want the reader to take, make it easy for them to do so by providing them with a clear call to action in the form of a 'Buy now' or a 'Contact us' button they can click to book an appointment or request more information.

What language does your reader use?

Using the client avatar's vernacular is vital for effective communication and is a form of localisation, which, as a translator, you will be familiar with. As a mother tongue British English speaker, I am aware that U.S. English is different, so if my audience is in the U.S. or is international, I need to ensure that the target text reflects this. For example, in the U.K. we call 'French fries' 'chips', whereas in the U.S., 'chips' are what we call 'crisps' in the U.K. If I were to write copy for an American audience to promote 'crisps' I would need to call them 'chips' otherwise they would be confused.

Similarly, if my client avatar is 25 and male, I need to find out what language they are using and what resonates with them so that they feel that the copy is talking to them and targets their pain points and provides the perfect solution to their problem.

There are now so many ways to do this, with all the different types of media now available:

- Reading what they read online
- Follow people who match your client persona on social media
- Pick up on the language they use to communicate with each other in the comments section and finding out how they feel about specific issues
- Listen to podcasts they might listen to
- Watch TV shows aimed at that demographic
- Observe friends, family or colleagues who fall under the same demographic

Find a way that works best for you to access and absorb the language they use and what matters to them and your copy will be more effective by resonating with them in their language.

Chapter 7
Ripping up the rules

"The person who follows the crowd will usually go no further than the crowd."
Albert Einstein

Ripping up the rules: time to forget grammar

As a translator, you may find this section alarming initially, and of course, you can't ignore grammar completely in copywriting. However, what you can do is break grammar rules for effect in the following cases:

- To emphasise a point
- When it is appropriate for the target audience
- To be more engaging
- To create a catchy strapline or slogan
- To match a brand's identity and personality

An excellent example of this is the case of the 'Beanz Meanz Heinz' slogan that we talked about in Chapter 5. Here it is clear to the audience that the 'z' at the end of 'Beanz' and 'Meanz' is done for effect because Heinz ends in 'z' and not because the copywriter can't spell. It captures the reader's attention because the spelling is irregular and then impresses the reader with how clever it is as a play on words. The effect is to put the product front and centre of your mind when you think of baked beans.

Younger audiences who have grown up using text language and shortened forms, not to mention emojis, are more likely to feel more in touch with a brand that speaks in their voice, even if it breaks grammar rules.

McDonald's captured this in their tagline 'i'm lovin' it', which helped relaunch the brand in 2003. This tagline does not capitalise "I" and uses an apostrophe at the end of 'lovin' instead of 'g'. More than twenty years later, the world-renowned global fast-food chain is still using it because it works, appeals to its target younger audience and represents the brand perfectly.

When else can you forget grammar in copywriting?

Besides the situations mentioned above, if you're copywriting in English, you can also start and end sentences with prepositions. Starting a piece of copy with "And" or "But" can create a sense of urgency and be more engaging for the reader. It makes the brand appear bold and not afraid to ignore grammar conventions to get its point across. You can also use punctuation more freely to make a point, such as a double or triple question mark or exclamation mark used to create a dramatic effect, such as in the sentence "Beat that!!!" or "Say what???".

Despite the luxury of having some artistic licence in copywriting, be wary of breaking too many rules for fear of appearing ignorant of standard grammar rules and conventions. Break the rules sparingly and effectively; such copy will have more impact, but don't abuse the reader's good nature. As a translator, it may take a while to shake off the shackles that grammar has unwittingly restricted you with for many years. However, based on my personal experience, you will feel remarkably liberated and free to write without constraints. Less is more, and copywriting is not a writing form that requires reams of perfect prose. It is a medium of effective communication where being concise and using target language is critical. One way of describing copywriting is using the spoken word in written form.

Welcome to AIDA

AIDA is a tried and tested formula used by copywriters to persuade prospects to buy. It is an acronym that stands for Attention, Interest, Desire and Action. Unless you are a marketing translator or have a background in marketing, you've probably never heard of AIDA, but it is a vital component of copywriting and ensures that your copy achieves the desired effect.

Let's explore each AIDA step and see how to apply it in practice.

A is for grabbing ATTENTION

The first thing you must do in copywriting is attract the reader's ATTENTION. This is usually done by using a great headline or in the case of a marketing email, an intriguing subject line. Advertising and copywriting legend David Ogilvy has claimed that 70% of sales are determined by the strength of the headline alone. So, make sure you don't skimp on your headline! While this statistic is hard to prove, the importance of headlines in capturing attention is a long-held belief and guiding principle in copywriting.

How to write a killer headline

David Garfinkel, the well-respected copywriter whose podcast I mentioned in Chapter 5, has written a book dedicated to writing headlines titled *Advertising Headlines That Make You Rich*.[6] In this book, he highlights the importance of writing great headlines that capture attention and draw readers into the copy. He provides tips for writing effective headlines that include ensuring your headline has an attention-grabbing hook, the use of powerful words to make an emotional connection with the reader, the use of specific language to avoid any ambiguity for the reader and outlining the benefits of the product/service.

One of the best headlines ever written is ascribed to David Ogilvy, an advertising genius who wrote the ad copy for a successful campaign for Rolls-Royce in the 1950s. The copy read:

> *"The loudest thing about this new Rolls Royce is its clock"*

His headline expertly highlights the exceptional craftsmanship, attention to detail and driving experience in each Rolls Royce car, illustrating this vividly using an unexpected detail. The campaign contributed to elevating the Rolls Royce brand and reinforcing its position as the world's leading luxury car manufacturer.

I is for sparking INTEREST

AIDA is a process, and once you have grabbed someone's attention, you need to gain their INTEREST. Once you have pulled the reader in with a compelling headline, you can generate their interest by outlining the **benefits** of your product or service.

To identify the benefits of a product or service, you need to put yourself in the customer's shoes and consider their needs, goals, desires and challenges and how the product or service you are promoting solves their problem or satisfies their needs. Consider the features of the product. For example, a fan might work at a particular speed, consume little energy, and emit very little noise. These are features. The benefits of these features are effective cooling power, energy and money savings and the fan is quiet enough to sleep through.

Unique selling points

In order to stand out from the competition, it is crucial to identify the unique selling points of the product or service you are selling. In the case of the fan, it may be that it is the quietest fan on the market. This sets it apart from other fans on the market and can be sold by focusing on the benefits of an ultra-quiet fan for the user. With each feature, you need to ask yourself the question, "So what?". If a fan is quiet, why does it matter? As mentioned above, this feature can be a significant benefit if you are looking for a bedroom fan and want to avoid being woken up by the noise of a fan throughout the night. There are multiple benefits to getting a good night's sleep, which can be emphasised in the copy.

Emotional and social benefits

Some products or services make the buyer feel socially successful and have an emotional benefit. Think back to the example of the Rolls Royce; someone who buys a Rolls Royce will feel superior to their peers and more confident and part of an elite group of fellow Rolls Royce owners. Social status matters to people, so if the product or service you are promoting provides a status benefit, be sure to include it in your copy.

Harness the power of reviews and testimonials

One of the best ways to find out how a buyer will feel after buying a particular product or service is by reading reviews and testimonials that offer priceless insights into why the customer made the purchase, what problem they were trying to solve and how they felt afterwards. You can also read the language typical customers use and weave statements into your copy. For example, a review for a locksmith might read:

> "Excellent, friendly service. Arrived quickly and replaced the lock so I could get back in the warm".

In just 17 words, you can tell that good service matters to someone who needs an emergency locksmith. It's also essential that they are friendly. The customer trusts this person to access their house, so being trustworthy is paramount. Another plus point is the speed at which they arrived and fixed the lock. A fast response time is vital if someone is locked out late at night or on a cold day.

Here's an example of how you could write website home page copy for a locksmith, focusing on the benefits based on that one review alone:

Fast reliable service, delivered by your friendly local locksmith. You can rely on us to get you back in your home with a warm cup of tea in your hand in superfast time.

The D in AIDA is for DESIRE

Once you have the reader's ATTENTION and INTEREST, your job is to make the reader want to buy. You can do this by planting the seed of DESIRE by describing a vision of their new life after the purchase, when they are now relieved of the problem they are currently experiencing. You can spark the necessary desire by appealing to the reader's needs, emotions or aspirations.

Ensure you highlight the positive outcomes of buying the product or service in your copy and demonstrate how your product or service can fulfil their desires or even solve their problem. Another tip to pique desire is to create a sense of urgency or exclusivity with a time-limited or number-limited offer. Testimonials and reviews are great for backing up claims in your copy, increasing the audience's engagement and for adding social proof, as they provide first-hand accounts of users' experiences.

Now it's A for ACTION

Once you have caught their ATTENTION, sparked their INTEREST and created the DESIRE to buy, you need to encourage them to take ACTION.

This is usually done with a 'CALL NOW' or 'GET IN TOUCH HERE' or 'GET A QUOTE' call to action. The whole point of the copy is to prompt the reader to do something. This action may vary, from making a purchase to requesting information or signing up to a mailing list. Whatever action you want the reader to take, make sure it is explicit and easy for them to do.

Keywords and why they matter

There are two reasons why keywords are important.

1 They add relevance to the copy and industry you are writing for so Google can match people's searches with your content.
2 They are great for SEO (search engine optimisation) and ranking on Google, which means you can be found by people who are specifically seeking your product or services.

If you are writing copy for publication online, on a website for example, you will need to use keywords to ensure that search engines and their users can find the copy. The best way to do keyword research is by using a keyword tool such as Google's Keyword Planners, Mangools or Semrush. There are many others on the market, so research and find a product that works best for you. Some offer free research, while others charge.

Writing a brief

As a translator, you are probably more familiar with receiving a brief than writing one. In my experience, translation briefs are less informative than copywriting briefs, often being little more than a purchase order. In copywriting, however, you need to take the lead and scope out the project back to the client, detailing enough time to conduct your competitor, client and industry research.

What to include in your brief

A copywriting brief outlines the essential details of a copywriting project. It details the client's needs regarding copy and ensures that both parties know what to expect from the finished product. If you're lucky you may receive a detailed brief from the client, but often you need to produce one yourself. This becomes an essential safeguard upfront, ensuring you have written proof of what has been agreed with the client, and the time (and cost) needed to complete it. So, if you are writing your own copywriting brief, make sure it includes the following information:

Project overview: Provide a brief overview of the project, including the type of copy that is needed, the target audience and the desired outcome.

Target audience/client avatar: This refers to the group of people you are trying to attract with your copy. It is vital that you understand the target audience's needs, wants and pain points to write copy that resonates with them.

Tone of voice: Specify the intended tone of voice for the copy. This could be authoritative, professional, conversational, informal, humorous, friendly, etc.

Key messages: These are the main points, the key benefits or unique selling points that you want to communicate in your copy. They should be clear, concise, and persuasive or accurate, depending on the purpose of the copy.

Call to action: This is what you want the reader to do after they have read your copy. It could be visiting a website, signing up for a newsletter or making a purchase.

Deadlines: Don't forget to set deadlines for the project so that everyone knows when things need to be completed.

Medium: Identify the medium in which the copy will be used, e.g., a website, an ad, a brochure, a social media post or an email campaign.

Competitors: Identify three main competitors and their messaging strategies. This will help you to understand the market context and differentiate the brand or product.

Supporting materials: List any relevant materials the client needs to provide that will help you write the copy, such as product descriptions, existing marketing materials, testimonials, internal policies such as a Code of Ethics, the company's mission statement or research data.

These materials can provide valuable insights and help you to write compelling copy.

Price: Make sure the price you quote allows for the time it will take you to do your research, write the copy and achieve the goals set. How many rounds of review will you include in the price and is there a deadline for requesting changes? Personally, I offer two free rounds of review, as there are invariably minor tweaks that the client wants to make to the first draft. After two rounds of review an additional charge is applied for subsequent rounds. I also find it useful to state that changes can only be made up to 28 days after submission of the work, to avoid clients taking too long to come back to me. When this does happen, I have already moved on and the project is no longer fresh in my mind, and it takes time to refamiliarise myself with the details of the project.

Crucial differences between copywriting and translating

I hope you have found this section useful and now feel that you understand the basics of copywriting. This book is not intended to be a definitive guide or textbook for copywriting. As I mentioned in previous chapters, there are plenty of books on the theory of copywriting and courses available online and in person that I recommend you take to hone your skills.

The intention of this book is to enable you as a translator to pivot your business and add another income stream while leveraging your existing written skills. The purpose of this section, therefore, is to highlight the differences and similarities between operating as a freelance translator and a freelance copywriter, because although there is much common ground, there are also crucial differences in writing style and approach that you need to be aware of to communicate effectively as a copywriter.

Tasks to complete

2. Take a favourite brand or your own business and identify your client avatar and tone of voice

3. Gather psychographic information on your client avatar

4. Create a buyer persona and outline their typical day

5. Write a strapline of a favourite brand or your own company that breaks grammar rules for effect

6. Write 300 words of Home page copy for a website for an imaginary or existing company, that follows the principles of AIDA

7. Create a copywriting brief template and complete it for an imaginary project

COPY THAT!

Part four

COPY THAT!

Chapter 8
Ready to launch

Carpe diem!

Launching as a copywriter

If you have followed all the steps in the previous chapters, you are now ready to start trading as a copywriter. This may feel daunting, and you may well be suffering from a lack of confidence, often described as imposter syndrome, but you *must not* let that hold you back. Take courage from the fact that by now you have:

- Completed a copywriting course
- Become a regular listener of copywriting podcasts
- Started following professional copywriters on social media
- Started reading and consuming ads differently
- Practised writing copy for your own business or that of a friend or colleague
- Honed your excellent transferable writing skills gained as a translator
- Learnt how to identify the correct tone of voice
- Learnt how to create a buyer persona
- Understood when you can bend grammar rules for a specific effect
- Understood how to prepare a brief

This means that you are now fully equipped to offer copywriting services. Let me repeat that in case there is still a voice in your head saying you are not ready: **YOU ARE NOW FULLY EQUIPPED TO OFFER COPYWRITING SERVICES.**

How to find your first client

There are many ways you can find your first client, and each route to market comes under the umbrella term of marketing. It is now time to apply what you have learnt about copywriting and start marketing yourself as a professional copywriter. To do that, firstly, you need to identify who your ideal client is.

You can do this by answering the following questions:

- Which industry do you want to service?
- Who is the decision-maker in the organisation/company?
- Do you prefer working with a particular type of person or business? E.g., coaches, creatives, therapists or lawyers, for example.
- What kind of content do you want to write, e.g., sales letters, blogs, thought-leadership articles?
- What size company do you want to work for? Solopreneurs or SMEs?

B2B or B2C

You may or may not be familiar with the terms B2B and B2C. Simply put, B2B means business-to-business and B2C means business-to-consumer. Let's look at some practical examples of B2B and B2C copywriting clients.

Suppose you want to work for SaaS (software as a service) providers that create software to help a business run more efficiently. In that case, your ideal client is B2B, as they are a business providing services to other businesses. If, on the other hand, you would prefer to sell copywriting services to companies that sell to consumers and are B2C, for example, therapists, then you need to target them accordingly in your marketing.

Let's now examine the different forms of marketing you can use to be found online by prospective clients and how you can actively seek out and sell to your ideal clients.

Social media marketing

In the digital age that we live in, it is essential that you are visible online and leverage social media to promote yourself and the services that you offer. As a B2B copywriter, I use LinkedIn to market my services and find it very effective. If you don't have a LinkedIn profile, or if your profile is hopelessly out of date, I recommend you start by updating your profile and describing yourself as what you want to be in 12 months' time. For example, if you are a legal translator and feel very comfortable writing for that profession, you may want to write copy for solicitors and legal practices. In that case, I suggest you call yourself 'a copywriter for the legal profession' in your profile.

The next step is to generate varied, relevant content to build an audience, credibility and authority. Talk about industry articles and what your stance or opinion on them is. Don't forget to show some personality and talk about your day-to-day work. People buy from people, even if they are buying on behalf of a company or organisation.

Also, remember to demonstrate your knowledge and proficiency in the sector you want to serve. The best way to do this is by writing regular blogs and articles, or a case study about a client that you have helped overcome a specific topic; plus share testimonials and reviews. A great way to gain engagement is to create polls from time to time to find out what your clients want from a copywriter and then strategically target your content and marketing to match their needs.

Which platform is best for you?

It is crucial to find the right social platform/s for your new business and learn how to leverage it/them to market yourself. Invest time researching the different social media platforms to find your ideal clients.

If you intend to do mostly B2C copywriting, Facebook or Instagram are probably best for you, or even TikTok. If you're still unsure which platform/s to focus on, hire a social media strategist and get professional advice. The most important thing is that you are present on the platform that your ideal clients are on and that you provide fresh, relevant content that is of value to your audience. And yes, that does include regularly posting video content if you want to stay ahead of the curve. If that makes you uncomfortable, I suggest not overthinking it and just start making a few videos. You don't even need to publish them initially. Just get used to speaking to the camera naturally and comfortably.

Another crucial aspect to bear in mind when using social media for business purposes is that, just like when you use social media for personal interactions, it is **sociable** (the clue is in the name!). This means that you need to engage with your audience and followers and not simply post and walk away. By engage, I mean replying to their comments on your posts and liking and commenting on other people's posts. To build an audience of trusted followers who will one day feel they can refer business to you, social media activity needs to be embedded in your daily routine.

Digital marketing

Digital marketing is now the most effective way to find clients. So, what is it, and how do you use it? Digital marketing encompasses all forms of marketing using digital technologies, i.e. search engines, SEO, content marketing, email marketing, etc.

If you already have a website for your translation business, you can add another page to your services or create a dedicated landing page just for copywriting. You can ask an SEO specialist about pay-per-click ads or search engine optimisation to help generate leads and grow your new business. If you don't have the budget to pay for SEO services, it's still worth having a website, as it provides credibility and is a platform to showcase your skills and services. Don't forget that, along with a good LinkedIn profile, the best marketing tool you have for your copywriting services is your website!

Another route to market is by registering with an online freelancing platform that allows copywriters to pitch for work, such as Upwork. As an experienced translator this didn't appeal to me as a route to market, so I have no personal experience to draw on, as most of my work comes from referral marketing.

Referral marketing through networking

Referral marketing involves you joining a group of fellow business owners from different professions and building strong relationships with them over time. Once you are well-known and trusted by each other, you will start referring clients to each other.

Networking has been the single most effective way for me to find new clients as a copywriter and I highly recommend it, which is why I have dedicated the whole next section, Part Five, to discussing the different ways you can network to find new clients and how to make it work for you.

Asking for testimonials/reviews

When I launched as a copywriter, the first thing I did was join a networking group. This decision was instrumental in me securing my first few clients. I then wrote a blog for one of the long-standing members who was also part of the leadership team. This meant that his opinion was highly respected within the group.

As I was new to copywriting and a member of the networking group, after having completed the assignment, I asked the member, if he was happy with it, if he would write me a testimonial and share it with the group. Fortunately, he was delighted with the blog and did not hesitate to write a testimonial for me and share it with the group. This was key to raising my profile among the members of the group and soon led to other referrals and offers of work from other members.

I recommend you join a networking group that suits your business goals as soon as possible and try to secure work from a trusted member of that group. If they are happy with your work, then you should ask them for a testimonial. This will help establish visibility and credibility within the group and hopefully lead to more referrals.

If you are not part of a networking group, it is still good practice to ask your clients to leave a review or write a testimonial for you to help future clients find out what it's like working with you.

Identify your brand

Whether you are aware of it or not, you are now a product and, as such, a 'brand' and can use your own marketing to show off your newly acquired copywriting skills. Look again at Part Three and identify your buyer persona and the tone of voice, pain points, benefits, problems that you solve, etc., so you can effectively market your brand.

Bear in mind that branding extends beyond tone of voice. It also encompasses brand colours, fonts, values and other aspects that create a brand personality.

To help identify your brand, you could work with a branding consultant or conduct research online to find out how to ensure that you have identified and understood your brand, and then you can make sure that it is presented consistently in all your marketing endeavours.

Develop your pricing structure

Before you start trading as a copywriter, make sure that you have determined how much your services will cost. In my opinion, one of the best ways to do this is to decide on an hourly rate that you feel is commensurate with your skills and experience. Don't forget to factor in the years you have spent studying, writing as a translator or other professional skills that you have acquired. It's also worth researching online what other copywriters charge by visiting their websites and measuring their level of skill and experience against your own.

Once you have figured out your hourly rate, then work out how long it will take you to research, plan and write commonly requested services such as a 1000-word blog or a 750-word landing page. For example, if you determine that your hourly rate is £50 and you calculate that it will take you 4 hours in total to write a 1000-word blog, then you should charge £200 for this service.

Some copywriters also offer a day rate, so you may prefer to work according to this model. Once you have fixed your prices for certain services, you can then either post them on your website (some people prefer to do this so that clients know what to expect to pay for their services) or you can withhold your rates and create bespoke quotes once you have determined the scope of the project. The choice is yours and it is wise to make sure you understand the full scope of a project before quoting a price to prevent scope creep. Scope creep can happen when you work with a new client, for example, and you need to invest more time researching their industry, client avatar, etc. so be sure to take this into consideration in when you are preparing your quote.

Productise your services with packages

Before you start engaging clients, you need to be clear on what you can offer them in terms of a solution to their copywriting problems. Of course, sometimes you will need to create a bespoke solution tailored to the client's specific needs, but generally, most clients will want help with website pages, case studies, newsletters and blogs.

Blogs are one thing that clients often need on a recurring basis, so it's a good idea to offer them a package of four or twelve blogs that they can buy, either by paying in a lump sum or on a monthly basis.

One advantage of packages that you create is that you have determined the scope and set the boundaries. This offers you a greater level of control over how the service is delivered and the lead times.

If you do create packages, always ensure that your packages are cheaper than paying for one-off pieces. For example, a 4-blog deal must be cheaper than four individual blogs, to incentivise the client to buy in bulk. Another idea is to create a blended package that is more of a pick'n'mix approach. Such a package could be structured in a way that the client can choose three out of a possible five pieces of copy such as:

- A blog
- A case study
- A landing page
- A refresh of a website page
- A newsletter

The trick is to ensure that what you offer in a pick'n'mix style package takes roughly the same amount of time to research, plan and write. That way it will be priced appropriately to recompense you for the time you spend writing it.

The importance of building a portfolio

To showcase the different types of content you can write, I recommend that you start building your portfolio right from the start, which means after you have written your first piece of copy. As your skills improve, you can edit it, but just like you would want to see samples of a builder's work, for example, before hiring them, clients will very likely ask to see samples of your work. It is then much easier to send them a collated version than trawl through various folders on your computer to look for the correct version of each piece of copy.

Using consistent messaging

Consistent messaging is vital to build a bridge that connects your brand with your ideal clients. Be clear in your intentions and reflect that in your copy. Go back and re-read about AIDA and apply it throughout your website copy, social media posts and any other blogs or promotional materials you produce.

By being consistent in your messaging, you will be able to build an audience that may initially follow you, and then, when the time comes, and they need a copywriter or someone they know does, they will think of you as you will have resonated with them. They will have a clear idea about where your strengths lie and be confident in your ability to solve their problem.

To niche or not to niche?

Initially, you may want to try writing for various clients and industries until you feel that you have found one that works for you, either for financial reasons or because you enjoy writing for that industry or sector. If you are a translator with extensive experience in a specific specialism such as tourism or pharma, it may well be a good strategy to stick to what you know and leverage the contacts and knowledge that you already have.

The question of when to niche is best answered: as soon as possible. Just as a marketing expert will advise you to niche down in translation, the same applies to copywriting and, just like in translation, you don't have to niche down to one specialism. For example, my copywriting niches are Property and Construction, and Aesthetics. It took me three years to identify my niches because, at first, I wanted to try writing for different types of clients and business sizes.

Initially, I thought my ideal clients were female solopreneurs, but I couldn't have been more wrong! The reason why targeting this group was not very successful for me is that female coaches tend to be very good at writing themselves. They are intuitive and empathetic and know who their target audience is, so essentially, demand for copywriters from this group is low. Also, as solopreneurs, their budget is relatively small, and copywriting is not essential or a pain point for them.

Next, I tried writing for tradespeople. This didn't work well either as most of their work comes from word of mouth and I found they didn't have the time to explain what they do or the inclination. Few of them even had websites and, what's more, they couldn't see the point in having one.

Fast forward a couple of years and I started writing for a local estate agent. Finally, here was a small, locally owned business that was time-poor, keen to stand out from the competition, understood the value of good copy and had a marketing budget. This is when I started to consider Property and Construction as a niche and started to visit networking groups targeting this industry.

Since then, I have worked for various companies in this sector, from facilities management to office fit-out and block management firms. One thing they have in common is that they are all in a very competitive market and need to differentiate themselves and stand out from the crowd. They have staff, but their staff are all over-stretched and skilled in trades such as surveying, construction, verbal selling, etc. What was key in this industry was that they all understood and appreciated the value of compelling, persuasive copy. So, far away from my original target ideal client, most business owners I now deal with as clients are male, very direct, clear about what they want to achieve with the copy or content and know whom they are selling to.

To sum up, in just over two years, my client avatar changed from female coaches to male business owners in the Property and Construction industry! The lesson here is to start with a plan of what your target market is, create your brand, establish the right tone of voice and who your target audience is but remain willing to adapt to suit the market or a niche that you evolve into. Don't be afraid of having more than one niche! As I have said, I currently have two: Property and Construction, and Aesthetics.

When you think about having a niche, I also recommend doing some market research and finding out which industries need and value copywriting and content creation. Then try to find an industry that is aligned with your skills, personal and professional values and financial goals.

Using humour in copy

Now that you have started consuming ads differently, you may have seen examples of copy in advertising campaigns that use humour to get a message across. An excellent example of this is provided on napkins served in Pret A Manger, a British-based takeaway coffee and snacks shop. The copy reads as follows:

> *"This napkin is made from 100% recycled stock (Pret's environment department is militant, we're making headway). If Pret staff get all serviette-ish and hand you huge bunches of napkins (which you don't need or want) please give them the evil eye. Waste not want not."*

Here the company uses its napkins to highlight its values and commitment to protecting the environment, yet without sounding too earnest or preachy. The copy is funny but enlightening, and who doesn't like to read while eating a sandwich or drinking a coffee?

Is it always appropriate to use humour? Absolutely not. Injecting personality is one thing and Pret has worked hard to define their tone of voice, brand guidelines and values and these are conveyed consistently throughout their copy. They also know their audience and are appealing to them with their messaging.

There is no doubt that humour is one of Pret's tone of voice descriptors but remember what we discussed in Part Three. Humour is a choice and can be part of a brand's tone of voice, but equally, if you are selling pensions or healthcare products, it may be entirely inappropriate to use humour, so please don't assume that it is unless your client has specified it as part of their tone of voice.

Managing your first client

You've finally arrived at that long-awaited day when your first potential copywriting client expresses an interest in you writing copy for them. But what should you do first?

The first thing you should do is have a 30-minute, free, discovery call with them either online using video conferencing software such as Teams or Zoom or talk to them over the phone or, if it's convenient, meet them face to face.

Why? To find out if you are a good fit for each other.

What to talk about on a discovery call

A discovery call is vital to work out if you and the prospective client can work well together and if you are the right person to solve their problem. If you are focussed in your discussion and strict about timekeeping – remember, this is a free, no-obligation service, so running over is going to cost you time - you should know by the end of the call whether you want to work with each other.

It took me a while to perfect what to discuss in a discovery call and I used to run over time and not ask the right questions. These days, I am very good at sticking to the following plan and find that it works well for the client and for me and is a very successful filtering system.

This is how I structure my discovery calls:

1. Ask what problem they want you to solve
2. Listen to their answer
3. Explain how you can help
4. Offer practical solutions
5. Explain what it's like working with you
6. Offer to prepare a quote

1. Ask what problem they want you to solve

This may sound obvious, but it isn't. It's very easy when a call starts to spend a long time discussing niceties such as the weather, a common trait of British people, or what you did over the weekend, but remember the clock is ticking and the best way to start the call is by saying something along the lines of "Hello, it's nice to meet you. Thanks for booking a discovery call with me. How can I help you with your copywriting?". Or something along those lines in your own words, but that isn't too verbose or distracting from the point of the call.

2. Listen to their answer

This one also took me some time to master. It's very easy to interrupt or interject if you feel you have something of value to add, but in this case, it pays just to listen actively and simultaneously plan your response regarding how you can help them solve their problem. Don't be afraid to be seen to be taking notes.

3. Explain how you can help

Once you have listened to their copywriting problem, explain to them how you, as an experienced copywriter, can help solve it. Tell them you understand why they need this copy and that you are happy to do it for them to save them the time and hassle of doing it themselves. Talk about your experience and explain why you are the right person for the job, provided that you believe you are, of course.

4. Offer practical solutions

Now is the time to tell them how you will solve their problem in practical terms. I recommend that you don't offer them more than a choice of two solutions, preferably with different price points, as any more can confuse the client. For example, if they need regular blogs for their website and social media, you can offer them a one-off package of 4 blogs or a 12-month blog package that they can either pay for upfront or pay monthly at a slightly higher rate.

5. Explain what it's like working with you (customer journey)

Once you have explained how you can help and have offered practical solutions to their copy needs, it's time to briefly talk them through your customer journey so they know what to expect if they choose to accept your quote. This should include payment terms, delivery schedules, approval deadlines, how many rounds of review you offer before incurring a charge, and anything else that you include in your service, such as a request for a review or testimonial after the job has been delivered.

6. Offer to prepare a quote

By now you should be coming to the end of the call. At this point, I ask the potential client if they would like me to prepare a quote based on the discussions that we have had and then they can decide if they want to proceed or not. You can also add a time limit or an offer to the quote so that you have a good reason to follow up with them. You might say, for example, "My prices are going up next month so if you book now or within the next XX days/weeks I can offer you the current price". Clients are generally happy for you to send a quote and that is when you should end the call, go away, write the quote and send it to them for approval.

You are now fully equipped to start seeking your first copywriting job. If you follow my suggestions, you will be in an excellent position to start trading as a copywriter and boost your income with a new revenue stream.

Chapter 9
The customer is not always right

"People will forget what you said, people will forget what you did, but people will never forget how you made them feel."
Maya Angelou

Dealing with a dissatisfied customer

We've all heard the phrase, "The customer is always right", but in reality, we all know that is not the case. In this chapter, we will explore how you manage sticky situations when the client questions or is dissatisfied with copy or content that you have created, and you need to respond.

If you are a translator, you will likely have been challenged over the years about stylistic and terminology choices that you have made and felt frustrated by having to justify to the client why you made the choice you did. You will no doubt have used your expertise and knowledge to show them that you made the right call.

As a translator, one of the most frustrating situations I come across is an end client who is not a native speaker of English and has questioned my grammar or terminology choices based on faux amis, word order or grammar rules in their own language (i.e., the source language), such as the use of 'they' in English when referring to someone of unknown gender. In contrast, French, for example, still favours the use of "il" meaning "he" to describe someone of an unspecified gender. This has been culturally unacceptable in English for decades and long before the mainstream use of the non-binary choice of pronouns which has become increasingly prevalent in recent years.

What can go wrong in copywriting

In copywriting, when I have experienced unhappy clients, it is usually down to the fact that they don't understand the basic premise of copywriting, which is to use a conversational, persuasive style of writing in a particular tone of voice and in language that the target audience uses and understands.

Remember what we learnt in Part Two from the book *Obvious Adams*. When the client questions the copy Obvious Adams has written, he replies, "Mr. Merritt, to whom are you advertising – paper makers or paper users?" Well, the same problem exists today due to a lack of understanding on the client's part regarding the concept of writing to sell.

One example from my experience is a garden centre I wrote the website copy for. Despite having done the necessary groundwork, as described in Part Three, the client was not happy with the first version of the copy because they felt that it didn't appeal to younger families as well as older people even though the client avatar that we had established together was as follows:

Client avatar

Malcolm – 55 years old, semi-retired, conservative, professional, comfortably off, loves spending time with grandchildren, watching the cricket, pottering in the garden, playing bowls, looks up to the royal family, loves his family and pleasing them, has a dog, worries about leaks and boiler cover.

In this case, I felt the client had missed the point, but I agreed to tweak the copy to appeal to a wider demographic. I did this by changing certain inferences I had made about Malcolm and his typical day. Below is the first version and below that is the final version of the copy that I delivered to the client:

First version

Find the perfect summerhouse for your garden

Would you like a private room in your garden where you can <u>escape the grandchildren and engross yourself in a good book, enjoy an ice-cold beer with an old friend or just appreciate your garden in peace</u>? Whatever *your reasons for wanting a summerhouse, we can help you find the perfect solution for your garden and ensure it is in keeping with your style and the architecture of your house.*

Final version

Find the perfect summerhouse for your garden

Would you like a private room in your garden where you can <u>sit and enjoy your morning coffee, work, play, read, entertain or just simply relax and unwind</u>? Whatever your reasons for wanting a summerhouse, we can help you find the right solution for your garden and ensure it is in keeping with your personal style and the architecture of your house.

In the first version, I have underlined the section that specifically targeted the original client avatar. The original client avatar, as a mature person, has more leisure time and is more likely to read books than listen to audiobooks or podcasts. As a male he will possibly like having a beer with an old friend and will find comfort and peace in a quiet garden. He may well have young grandchildren who visit regularly and make a lot of noise, so having a bolthole at the end of the garden will be of immense value to him.

In the final version, you can see that the copy has been tweaked to target a younger avatar without necessarily excluding Malcolm, but it is less targeted to his pain points and much vaguer. This was what the client wanted, so I changed it, but I think the first version is better than the revised version, given the original client avatar.

If you find yourself in this situation, I advise you to be clear when you write your brief about who you are targeting in the copy and why (which you share with the client from the outset) so that if your client requests changes, you can refer back to what was agreed before you started. It is normal for a client to request minor tweaks, but changing the client avatar is a major change so make sure you manage the client's expectations from the outset. Personally, I offer two free rounds of review. After that, any additional requests for changes are chargeable.

What to do when writing copy for a third party

One of the biggest challenges you will face is when you write copy for a third-party client. This could be a situation where a web designer or a graphic designer, for example, is coordinating a website build or an advertising campaign. They then hire you to write the copy element but prefer to liaise with the end client themselves. If you are a translator, this is the same as working for a translation agency, which you will undoubtedly be very familiar with. The translation agency sends you the work and the brief, and any queries you may have regarding terminology or any other issues are sent to the end client via the intermediary of the translation agency's project manager, who is your point of contact.

In the case of copywriting, I find this more challenging than in translation because the brief I receive, which, if I'm lucky, will include a buyer persona, tone of voice, features, benefits and pain points, is often far less detailed than a brief that I would have prepared myself. This lack of or skeletal set of information makes writing the copy harder. As one of my lecturers said while I was completing my master's degree in Translation, "Before you can translate, first you have to understand.". This also applies to copywriting. To be able to get inside the head of the person you are trying to appeal to, it is crucial to know as much about them as possible.

One way of tackling this problem is by sending the contractor who has hired you a copy of the questionnaire you usually ask your direct clients to complete. Here is the questionnaire I use that can act as a template for you to ensure you get all the information you need to write the copy.

New client questionnaire

Thank you for choosing to work with me as your copywriter. In order for us to get your copy just right you need to complete this questionnaire as fully as possible. The answers to these questions will help me research your business, industry and ideal client to ensure the copy truly resonates with them.

Section 1

Your business

1. What is the name of your business?

2. How long have you been trading?

3. What problem does your business solve for whom?

4. What are the main services that you offer?

5. What is your USP?

6. Are you B2B, B2C or both?

7. Who are your main customers?

8. How do most of your customers find you?

9. What are the features of your products/services?

10. What are the benefits of your products/services?

COPY THAT!

List your top 3 main competitors and provide a link to their websites

Competitor 1:

Competitor 2:

Competitor 3:

Your industry

Please provide as much information as possible about your industry, your positioning within it and the services you provide:

Copy strategy

1. Why do you need this copy?

2. What area of your business are you trying to improve with this copy?

3. What do you want your audience to do after they read the copy?

4. What are you trying to achieve overall with the copy? (E.g., attract new customers, build an online audience, generate new leads, drive conversions, or educate your audience about your products/services)

Establishing the right tone of voice and creating a client avatar

To create the right tone of voice for your website we need to establish your ideal client (avatar). Please answer the following questions so that we can do this:

1. What gender does your ideal client identify as?

   _____

2. What newspaper do they read?

   _____

3. How do they vote?

   _____

4. How old are they?

   _____

5. What job do they do?

   _____

6. What level of education do they have (left school at 16 or entered higher education)?

   _____

7. What type of programmes do they watch on TV? (sport, drama, documentaries, etc.)

   _____

8. What do they do in their free time?

_____

9. What are their goals?

_____

10. Who are their heroes?

_____

11. Who are their enemies?

_____

12. Who do they want to please?

_____

13. Who are they responsible for?

_____

14. Who might they let down or fail?

_____

15. What keeps them up at night?

_____

16. What is their name (think of a name or use one of your client's names i.e., Dave or Clare)?

_____

17 Describe their typical day below including where they live, their job, who they come home to and what they do in the evening.

E.g., John gets up at 7 o'clock, hops in the shower, gets dressed and takes the dog out for a walk. Then he comes back, eats breakfast, checks his email and dresses for work. He works in the office 2 days a week, and the other three days he works from home. In the evening he comes home, goes to the gym, cooks and eats dinner with his girlfriend and then they watch a drama series on TV before going to bed.

List of detailed tone descriptors

The tone of voice should reflect the experience your customers will have when working with you. To identify the correct tone of voice **please highlight approx. 6-8** of the following descriptors for your tone of voice:

1.	Authoritative	*20.*	Matter-of-fact
2.	Caring	*21.*	Nostalgic
3.	Cheerful	*22.*	Passionate
4.	Coarse	*23.*	Playful
5.	Conservative	*24.*	Professional
6.	Conversational	*25.*	Provocative
7.	Casual	*26.*	Quirky
8.	Dry	*27.*	Respectful
9.	Edgy	*28.*	Romantic
10.	Engaging	*29.*	Sarcastic
11.	Enthusiastic	*30.*	Serious
12.	Formal	*31.*	Smart
13.	Frank	*32.*	Snarky
14.	Friendly	*33.*	Sympathetic
15.	Fun	*34.*	Trendy
16.	Funny	*35.*	Trustworthy
17.	Humorous	*36.*	Unapologetic
18.	Informative	*37.*	Upbeat
19.	Irreverent	*38.*	Witty

Source: https://www.nngroup.com/articles/tone-voice-words/

Thank you for completing this questionnaire.

If you have any further information that you think will be of use, please provide it below.

The brief is so important!

To conclude, the best way to avoid disputes with clients or unhappy customers is to be as thorough as possible in the initial stages, especially when preparing the brief. At least then, if there is an issue, you can refer to the brief that the client signed off before you started the work, and you will have recourse to defend the decisions you have made in your copy.

So, as a single task to complete at the end of this chapter, draft your own client questionnaire, giving you that detailed brief you can refer back to, should a dispute arise.

Tasks to complete

1. Identify your target market/industry and decide whether you want to be a B2B or B2C copywriter

2. Determine which social media platforms best suit your business model

3. Identify your brand voice and values

4. Create social media accounts and profiles on your chosen platforms that reflect your brand

5. Determine your pricing structure, including packages

6. Decide whether you want to niche or not

7. Map out your future customers' journey

8. Create your own new client questionnaire

COPY THAT!

Part five

COPY THAT!

Chapter 10
How to network

"Dime con quién andas, y te diré quién eres"
["Tell me who you hang out with, and I'll tell you who you are."]

Networking: how to do it right

Let me begin this chapter by reminding you that, in my new venture as a copywriter, networking has been my *primary source* of clients, and therefore revenue, and, if you do it right, the same can apply to you. Now let's take a deep dive into how I leverage my network to attract new clients, what mistakes I have made along the way and what pitfalls I came across that I can help you avoid. Firstly, I'm going to start with how *not* to do it.

How not to network

As a translator, over the years I have attended various translation industry events and found them daunting, uncomfortable and awkward. I would turn up alone, grab a coffee and hide in the corner, invariably staring at my phone hoping nobody would approach me or, God forbid, talk to me! I would go networking and not network! As you can imagine this never resulted in any fruitful collaborations. Occasionally, I would talk to a couple of people and trade business cards, but with this approach I never reaped the rewards I had hoped for and so mostly I avoided it and therefore left money on the table.

My path to getting it right

Fast forward to 2019 and I am about to launch a new service offering copywriting services, but I need clients. Fortunately for me, my business coach was an experienced networker and invited me along to his weekly networking group, as they didn't have a copywriter and some of the business owners in the group needed my services. I was told to prepare a 60-second pitch outlining my services and what problems I could solve and for whom.

This all sounded doable until he told me that the meeting started at 6.45. Of course, at first, I though he meant 6.45 p.m. but no, the meeting actually started at 6.45 a.m. and was held at a seafront hotel in Eastbourne, which is a town on the south coast of England. Now, being more of a night owl than an early bird and having been a freelancer for twelve years and kept my own work hours, this seemed a ridiculous time to have a meeting, especially in England in winter. Did I mention the invite was for January, when the sun doesn't even rise until about 7.45 a.m. Anyway, determined to get this new arm of my business off the ground, I resolved to go to the meeting.

The day of the meeting finally arrived, and I got up at 4.30 a.m. to leave the house at 5 a.m. as it was about an hour and half's drive to the venue. If you've ever been to an English seaside town in January at six thirty in the morning, you'll know that it is freezing cold, very windy and VERY, VERY dark. Despite these challenges, I made it to the venue and was warmly received in the hotel reception by my business mentor and escorted to the meeting room. Needless to say, on arrival, I felt completely out of my comfort zone, out of my depth, and puzzled as to why I hadn't just made some excuse and stayed in bed instead.

My first networking meeting

As the meeting unfolded everyone enjoyed a hearty breakfast and then delivered their 60-second pitches describing what they do and the kind of business they were looking for. Everyone was friendly, seemed interested in what I did and asked me if I was interested in joining their group. This was nothing like the rather staid, somewhat stuffy, and less structured, networking events I had attended in the translation world. I thought the whole thing was fantastic, my adrenaline was flowing, and I took great delight in meeting everyone and hearing about what they did and how they had helped each other find clients by referring potential leads and clients to them. I was sold, I wanted to be a part of this group and help them find business and hopefully, in return they would want to do the same for me. So, I joined and forgot all about the travel challenges, the inclement weather and didn't even stop to consider if there was a similar group I could join nearer to home.

A steep learning curve

Gradually, over time I got to know people better and they started to understand the kind of services I offer and what problems I could solve. As my understanding of what they did and the kind of clients they were looking for became clearer to me, I started to get business.

By being in a group of diverse business owners who meet on a weekly basis I learnt a lot about how to network effectively. I built strong relationships with my fellow members and fine-tuned my 60-second pitch to be increasingly specific about the kind of clients I was looking for and how I could help them. Additionally, every week a member of the group would do a ten-minute presentation to explain more about who they are, their background, the services or products they offer and what kind of clients they are looking for. They would also provide tips on what to listen out for to help them find referrals. By pitching weekly and making this type of presentation every few months I soon became increasingly confident about describing my business and speaking to a roomful of people, which as I said, can be quite intimidating at first.

Know, like and trust

As any experienced networker will tell you, the referrals start to come when you tick all three of the 'know, like and trust' boxes. What do I mean by 'know, like and trust'? Well, first people need to get to know you. Obviously, when you are in a group that meets face-to-face you get to know each other much quicker than if you just meet every few months or once a year, as is often the case in translation networking. Next, people need to like you; nobody wants to help someone they don't know and don't like.

Lastly, for people to feel comfortable recommending you to their clients, they need to trust you to look after them and do a good job. Fellow networking group members will often test the services of other members before they refer them to someone they know, so that they don't damage their own reputation and the trust that they have built up with their clients, associates or friends and family.

Exploring different networking groups

Back to the story of my Eastbourne networking group. Did I mention that I joined this group in January 2020? Well, I'm sure you can remember what happened a couple of months later - the Covid-19 pandemic hit. As of 23 March 2020, the UK was put into lockdown and our weekly meetings moved online. As you can imagine, this wasn't so bad for me as I no longer had to get up so early and drive over an hour to the meeting.

Another plus point of our meetings moving online was that, as my networking group was part of BNI (Business Networking International), I could now attend the meetings of other groups up and down the country and worldwide. This was game-changing for me as now I could also use my membership to promote my translation services by attending meetings in countries that spoke the languages that I offered translation services for (French, Italian and Spanish) such as Spain, Italy, France and even Canada.

After having initially joined to sell copywriting services and with a virtual background for use on Zoom that only mentioned copywriting, I needed to re-brand. I couldn't turn up at an online meeting to promote my translation services with a copywriting virtual background. If my messaging wasn't clear, I could hardly tell other people theirs wasn't and convince them I could fix it. So, ARC Writing and Translation Services was born as a trading name of my limited company and became the message on virtual background. My client base soon started to expand and evolve.

Also, by networking in London groups, I was invited to other networking groups which eventually led to me joining a women-only networking group that was part of WIBN (Women In Business Network). Remember how I mentioned in Part Four that originally my ideal client avatar was female coaches/creatives?

Later that year, in October 2020, there was talk about going back to face-to-face weekly meetings, but I didn't want to travel all the way to Eastbourne, so I decided to join a local BNI group in Horsham. This worked well until at the end of 2022 when I decided to niche down into Property and Construction and re-focus my business towards the London market. This time I opted to join a BNI chapter in London (BNI refer to each of their networking groups as a chapter). I now felt that the type of businesses in my local group (mainly tradespeople) were not in contact with my target clients and I wasn't getting enough referrals to justify the time and money investment. This move was a wrench initially, as by now many of the members in my Horsham group were friends as well as network partners. However, it soon proved to be very successful in growing my business, by working closely with ideal referral partners and receiving better quality referrals.

Different networks you should join

You've heard my story and learnt what I did right and what I did wrong. Now let's explore the different types of networking you should do and why, based on my experience of networking.

- Network in your industry
- Network in your ideal client's industry
- Network with other business owners

Let's now look at each type of networking and examine why each is important.

Networking in your industry

As a translator, I am sure you understand the importance of networking in your industry. Firstly, it offers you the opportunity to meet fellow professionals and grow your network of contacts. Secondly, it enables you to gain insights into the latest trends, developments and technological advances. These can help you increase your productivity and speed up your workflow by adopting more efficient systems and process. Thirdly, you will often find service providers at industry events who provide services to help you run your business more smoothly, whether that is a CMS (content management system) specifically designed for members of your profession or SaaS (Software as a Service), for example, Memsource for translators.

The benefits of networking in your industry are obvious and plentiful, but it's not enough. You may have found that in translation your ideal clients were at networking events if they were project managers from translation agencies, but now that you are a copywriter you will need to network not only in the digital marketing space but outside of it, which leads us nicely into the next type of networking you need to do.

Networking in your ideal client's industry

If you recall, I explained in Chapter 8 that I have now niched down to being a copywriter for the Property and Construction sector, which means that to find my ideal clients I need to attend networking events specifically for people who work in or provide products or services for this industry. The benefit of this is that I am in front of decision-makers in that industry who would rather work with someone who understands their industry and has worked with someone or a company that they know. People buy from people, so if you attend networking events in your ideal client's industry regularly you will get into the 'know, like and trust' zone sooner and people in that network will start referring you to their contacts.

Networking with other business owners

Besides networking in your industry and in your ideal client's industry, it's also important to network with other business owners. By doing this you will gain support, feed off their positivity and learn about running a business by hearing about the different systems and processes that other small businesses owners employ, as well as learning what pitfalls to avoid. Most networking groups also have a regular flow of visitors and new members. This means that you have a constant stream of new people in your contact sphere who may need your services or know someone who does. You never know who other people know, and referrals can come from the most unlikely sources.

How to get maximum value from networking

As I mentioned above, I have been a member of BNI since 2020 and have learnt most of what I know about networking from being part of this well-organised global networking organisation. BNI provides training to help members who are new to networking on how to make the most of their membership and grow their businesses. I am not suggesting that you should join BNI; it doesn't work for everyone as it requires a significant financial and time investment, but it has worked well for me.

One of the things I personally like about BNI is its core values. I believe they are a key part of why BNI works for those whose values are aligned with those of the organisation and, when adhered to, they contribute to a group's success or failure. They essentially help to create the right culture in the group and provide consistency so that any group you visit, anywhere in the world, has the same meeting format so you know what to expect.

Let's examine BNI's core values and discuss why they matter:

1. Givers Gain®
2. Traditions & Innovation

3. Building Relationships
4. Lifelong Learning
5. Accountability
6. Positive Attitude
7. Recognition

Givers Gain®

There is a reason why this core value is top of the list. It is the value that underpins BNI's ethos: "If I give business to you, in return, you will want to give business to me". However, Givers Gain® goes further than that, as it is more about giving without expecting anything back in return and BNI's founder Dr Ivan Misner, considers it akin to the law of reciprocity, whereby if someone does something for you, you will feel obligated to do something for them in return.

Traditions & Innovation

This value is about having and honouring traditions whilst also keeping one eye on the future and being excited about how innovation can improve our lives and offer unforeseen opportunities for growth. An example of traditions in BNI would include having a visitor host dedicated to making visitors feel welcome and help them navigate the meeting and orient them afterwards to find out if they are interested in applying to become a member.

An example of innovation in a networking organisation would be when the global pandemic hit in 2020 and networking groups that had previously only met in person had to move online in order to continue to offer their members an opportunity to network. Most groups decided very quickly to move the weekly meetings online. Prior to this the idea of holding online meetings had always been dismissed because it was considered less effective than face-to-face networking. However, when the unforeseen happened and governments across the globe were imposing strict lockdowns on their populations, there was no other option than take the meetings online so that members could continue to benefit from their membership and support each through those challenging times.

Building Relationships

As we have discussed already, the most successful networkers build strong relationships with the people in their network. This is done by also meeting outside of scheduled meetings and having one-to-ones where you can get to know the other person on a deeper, more personal level by finding out about their interests, hobbies, family, etc. The better people know other people, the more likely they are to refer business to them.

Lifelong Learning

As a translator, you will understand the importance of CPD (continuing professional development) and this applies to all professions. If you are quite new to networking you should look to join a group that has resources that help members by providing a variety of in-person and online training courses to help members improve their networking skills and, therefore, get the most value out of their membership. All good networking groups should provide an opportunity for members to attend sessions on preparing a pitch, presenting, etc. to help members grow and develop and become effective networkers.

Accountability

One thing that sets BNI apart from other groups is the expectation and commitment to attend 50 weeks out of the year. If you can't make it one week because you are on holiday, too busy or unwell, you are expected to be represented by a substitute who will read out your pitch for you and listen to the other people in the group and feedback. This accountability part of the membership puts some people off, but it works for me and my personality. I have witnessed first-hand how damaging non-attendance is without good reason when you have joined a group that makes it clear from the outset that weekly attendance is expected. Not showing up without good reason or sending someone to stand in for you as a substitute (often referred to simply as a sub) sends an indirect message to the other members of the group that they are not important to you and that you can't be bothered to turn up and listen to what they have to say, especially if it is their turn to do their 10-minute presentation.

However, if you would prefer not to commit to regular attendance or your lifestyle does not lend itself well to this arrangement, a group that offers a more flexible approach to attendance will probably suit you better.

Positive Attitude

I love this core value! In the long, dark days of multiple lockdowns, turning up online to a meeting once a week and being surrounded by positive people was hugely uplifting. I distinctly remember attending an online BNI meeting during the pandemic in which one of the members spoke about how challenging his home life was due to members of his family being ill with Covid and coping with existing underlying health issues, and that attending his weekly BNI meeting and being infused with everyone's positivity was what kept him going all week. It was very moving and powerful.

It's also important to have a positive attitude in normal times and in face-to-face meetings. A negative attitude can be infectious as much as a positive one and can lower everyone's mood and the morale within the group.

Recognition

As in everyday life, when someone achieves highly or goes above and beyond, it's important to recognise their efforts. Effective networking groups do this in a variety of ways through notable networking awards, regional award ceremonies and testimonials. This makes the person being recognised feel valued and can help encourage people to raise their game and be the best version of themselves by creating a healthy spirit of competition.

Different forms of networking

There are several forms of networking available these days that range from structured weekly in-person groups to informal events and groups that you can attend on an ad hoc basis. In my experience, the more commitment that is required of members, the stronger the relationships that are formed and the sooner members start to receive referrals.

Since the Covid-19 pandemic there has been a huge increase in the number of online networking groups and an acceleration of the mainstream use of video conferencing platforms such as Zoom and Microsoft Teams that offer a convenient time-saving alternative to in-person networking. In addition to face-to-face and online networking there are also hybrid groups that alternate their meetings between face-to-face and online meetings, which have proved to be very popular as they provide an opportunity for regular face-to-face contact, once a month in person and three times a month online, for example, combined with the convenience of online networking.

Of course, there are also unstructured, informal networking events where people in an industry or sector meet, talk and network openly. In my opinion, all types can be effective if you work the room properly, which may mean following a strict agenda or just talking to people and finding out more about what they do. Whatever the format, networking is not the time to oversell yourself or sell yourself to the people you meet. It involves a lot more than simply handing out your business card or connecting on LinkedIn. It's about relationship building and training your own personal 'sales force' who can recommend your services to the people in their network.

Ideal referral partners and how to identify them

Another thing I have learned from networking is that it is important to build strong relationships with your ideal referral partners to find referrals for each other. An ideal referral partner is someone in your network who serves similar clients to you but offers a different or complementary service, so they are not a direct competitor.

An example of ideal referral partners for me as a copywriter who specialises in website copy would be a website designer, a graphic designer, a photographer, a videographer or anyone else who is involved in servicing or building websites. Ideal referral partners can often be found in your networks, and you should actively seek them out and engage with them so you can help each other grow your businesses.

Non-referral networking

Other networking events and groups exist that don't place any expectation on members to find referrals for one another. Before you invest in a networking group make sure you have thought about which format is best for you, your business goals and your schedule. If you spend long periods of time away from home, then a local networking group that expects you to attend regularly or find a substitute to represent you is unlikely to work for you.

Many people I know have successfully grown their business by joining non-referral networking groups. The advantages of this model are flexible attendance and no expectations to do anything for your fellow members outside of the meetings, such as find referrals for them or have one-to-ones. The downside is that it takes longer to build relationships with other members and for them to fully understand what you do and the kind of business you are looking for. You will therefore receive fewer referrals and have a weaker network support system.

Teams that serve the same clients

Some networking organisations form sub-groups of the networking group, or several networking groups that are part of the same organisation, that meets less frequently than the main group and comprises people who offer similar, complementary services. Essentially it is a group of ideal referral partners. Examples of such a team could be a legal team, a financial services team or a marketing team.

In practice, teams that serve the same clients offer members an opportunity to find ways of working together, possibly by offering a unified approach or package or just finding out how they can find referrals for the other members by gaining deeper insights into what the other members do.

Who should you book one-to-ones with?

One-to-one meetings are highly effective at helping you build and strengthen your relationships with members of your network. Initially, you should book one-to-ones with people who are potentially ideal referral partners for you, but also anyone who works in your niche. It's also a good idea to book a one-to-one with any visitors to your group, as you never know who they know and how they might be able to help you and vice versa until you have a focussed conversation alone with them.

Do make sure that you spend 50% of the one-to-one talking about each other's business and your ideal referrals and avoid just talking about one of you. If this does happen, I suggest booking another meeting so that you can discuss the person's business who didn't get the opportunity to explain what they do the first time round.

LinkedIn: the world's largest business network

They say New York is the city that never sleeps. Well, LinkedIn is the networking equivalent. It is always open for business and people login and access it across the globe 24 hours a day/seven days a week. If you haven't already created a profile on LinkedIn, I strongly recommend that you do, for the following reasons, even if you are offering B2C (business-to-consumer) services:

1. Company decision-makers use it regularly
2. Fast and easy way to message your contacts without clogging up your email inbox
3. It has over 100 million users worldwide
4. It can drive traffic to your website
5. It is good for SEO

How to make LinkedIn work for you

LinkedIn is the largest professional network in the world. But, like any network, you need to work at it. That means posting engaging, relevant content! But you're now an expert at generating good copy, right? Here is a starter list to consider:

- A comment on industry trends
- Updates about your company
- Personal stories
- Content that informs or educates your audience
- Content that helps users and stimulates interesting discussions

- Polls to help you understand your audience better and what their needs are so that you can target your marketing and services to meet their needs
- Showcase testimonials
- Post blogs

If you are stuck for what to post, there are articles online that can help you with ideas. Alternatively, you can hire a LinkedIn trainer or follow LinkedIn trainers, as they post relevant tips and tricks, especially regarding new platform features and what to post.

The main thing is to post regularly, ideally three to five times a week and comment on other people's posts and respond to comments in your posts. If you actively engage with people that you are connected to, and even those who you aren't, you will see your audience grow and you will start to receive business. Remember to tag people and organisations and use relevant hashtags to be found organically from people's searches.

One of the best stories I have heard about LinkedIn was a lady I know who runs a translation agency in India. She was contacted by someone who neither of us were connected to, following a post of mine that they had found organically on LinkedIn. My post was about a global BNI languages power team that I had just joined. The person that contacted her then went on to become a client. That is the power of LinkedIn! I have received work as a direct result of posting regularly and demonstrating not only knowledge and authority in my field, but also a bit of my personality.

Key reasons to network

Here is a summary of the main reasons *why* you should network:

- Find clients
- Receive referrals
- Learn from other business owners

- Grow your contact sphere
- Develop professionally
- Improve your presentation/public speaking skills
- Receive support from fellow members
- Learn about industry updates
- Grow your business

What makes a good networker?

A good networker will do the following things consistently:

- Attend every meeting or send a substitute
- Be prepared, have their pitch scripted or clear in their mind
- Dress appropriately, don't show up in tracksuit bottoms unless you are a personal trainer
- Wear a name badge - this helps visitors and subs to know who you are
- Arrive on time and stay until the end of the meeting
- Give 100% of their attention, not constantly checking their phone, make people feel important by listening to them
- Follow up on referrals they receive
- Track their referrals and who they received them from so that they can measure how effective each networking group is
- Help fellow members grow their business through referrals, testimonials and inviting people to join who are a good fit

What to include in your pitch?

As a networker, a 60-second pitch, also known as an elevator pitch, is a concise and compelling way to introduce yourself. It is also an opportunity for you to showcase your expertise and spark the interest of your listeners. Here's my advice on what you should include in your pitch:

1. Introduce yourself. State your name and your professional background or area of expertise. Make sure you keep it brief and relevant to the context of networking.
2. Start with a strong opening. Try to grab the listener's attention with a memorable and engaging statement or question to set the tone for the rest of your pitch.
3. Address your ideal client's pain points, whether this is being time poor or in genuine pain if you are an osteopath for example.
4. Highlight your value proposition. State the unique value you offer. Focus on your specific skills, knowledge or experience that make you stand out from your competitors. Emphasise how you can help others or solve their problems.
5. Share a recent testimonial. Mention a success stories or recent accomplishment that demonstrates your expertise and credibility. This will help you to build trust and confidence in your abilities.
6. Briefly explain who your ideal clients or partners are. This will help your fellow networkers understand the type of opportunities or connections you are seeking.
7. State your objective. Clearly articulate your networking goal or what you hope to achieve from attending the meeting or being part of the group. This could be finding new clients, looking for ideal referral partners or expanding your professional network.
8. Offer a call to action. End your pitch with a clear request or call to action. Here it is really important to be specific: you could ask for an introduction to a person in a company you would like to work for or asking for referrals in a certain industry. The main thing here is to make it easy for the listener to take the next step.

It can be hard to fit all these things into 60 seconds, but it can be done through practice and focussing on the key messages you want to convey that week. For example, one week you might want to talk about a new service you are offering and explain who it would benefit and why. Another week you might want to explain what it's like working with you by describing your customers' journey. The more you do it, the better you will get at it. Here is an example of my elevator pitch that I use when I am subbing or I give to people who are standing in for me to read out in the meeting.

Hi, I'm Antoinette Chappell from ARC Writing and Translation Services

I'm a freelance copywriter and translator. I write copy for companies that need to define what they do and stand out from the competition **in writing** *but don't have the time or inclination to do it themselves, or maybe writing is simply not their thing.*

I help promote businesses by writing copy for websites, brochures, and email marketing campaigns, among other things. My USP is that I have nearly 15 years of experience working as a professional translator and copywriter, so I don't just know one language, but four.

All my clients benefit from ad hoc, creative copywriting when they need it – without unnecessary overheads when they don't. I give them peace of mind by getting essential copy tasks off their to-do list and out in the marketplace where it can work for them.

I am looking for business owners who would like to find out how copywriting can make their business stand out from the crowd.

Antoinette Chappell, **ARC Writing and Translation Services**

HELPING YOU GET YOUR MESSAGE ACROSS

Practise and refine your pitch. Once you have drafted your pitch, practise delivering it in a concise and confident manner. Time yourself using the stopwatch app on your phone or another device to ensure you can deliver it in the timeframe given. In most networking groups this is 60 seconds, but other networks may have variations on this, 40 seconds for example. Refine and re-write it based on how well it was received and if anyone took action.

Final note on networking

Networking is a long game; it takes a huge time and energy investment to make it work, so if you're looking a quick solution, networking is not it. You may be lucky and attend one meeting and get a referral, but this is not usually the case. It takes time to build relationships and enter the 'know, like and trust' zone.

Also, bear in mind that you are not selling to the room but educating your sales force (this is how to think of the fellow members of your referral networking group) about what problems you solve and for whom. This means that when they are out and about and they hear someone describe the problem you solve they will refer them to you. If you have trained your fellow members effectively, they will know exactly who to refer to you. For example, in my case I tell my fellow network members to listen out for people who are having a new website built and are complaining about not having the time to write the copy. These people are a great referral for me as copy is often one of the last things to be done on a website and everyone thinks they can save money by doing it themselves, but they haven't got a clue where to start. This is where I can come in and help get this essential task off their to-do list.

In three and a half years I've come a long way since that cold, windy morning in January driving to Eastbourne. I still believe I am on a networking journey and continue to explore different groups and opportunities. In the past six months I have:

- Been a weekly member of a London BNI chapter
- Subbed at various other chapters
- Joined a global BNI language power team

- Subbed at a WIBN group
- Attended several informal open networking events in the Property and Construction sector in London and Brighton
- Joined a networking group that offers mixed events (social, structured, speed networking, etc.)
- Attended the ELIA Together translation conference in Rome
- Attended Atomicon, a digital marketing conference in Newcastle
- Regularly posted and engaged with others on LinkedIn.

Difference between networking groups and conference networking

You'll notice from the list above that I attended two networking conferences this year. One dedicated to the translation industry and one for the digital marketing industry. Despite being for different industries and audiences they had a similar format: keynote speeches, talks and seminars, interspersed with opportunities to network. These networking opportunities were generally before or after the talks, in the form of coffee breaks or a meal and/or drinks in the evening when delegates were given the opportunity to mingle and network with fellow attendees.

I made some new connections at both events and have connected with the people I met on LinkedIn as well as the speakers who I found delivered interesting and relevant content. Some delegates attended in groups comprising people they already know in their area and with whom they travel to and from the event, whilst other people meet up with people they already know but haven't seen for a while, either due to time or geographical constraints.

To conclude, these events are worth attending because of the industry updates and different perspectives you are exposed to during the talks and to make new connections with other people who work in your industry that could go on to refer work to you and vice versa.

COPY THAT!

I hope that that demonstrates the variety of networking events that you need to attend to be an effective networker and that you now understanding why each networking event you attend matters. Buckle up and brace yourself for your networking journey, and I hope you enjoy it as much as I am enjoying mine!

Tasks to complete

1. Research networking groups in your area

2. Write an engaging and specific 60-second pitch

3. Visit an in-person networking group

4. Attend an online networking meeting

5. Book one-to-ones with ideal referral partners

6. Create a profile on LinkedIn and commit to posting 3-5 times a week

7. Engage with your audience and other people on LinkedIn

8. Find out about networking conferences coming up in your industry or that of your ideal client

COPY THAT!

Part Six

COPY THAT!

Chapter 11
Copywriting and AI: what the future holds

"Evolve or die"
Charles Darwin's Theory of Evolution

ChatGPT: my initial introduction

At the first meeting of my weekly networking group after the Christmas break in January 2023, I was chatting to the group's digital marketing representative during open networking prior to the start of the meeting and he asked me if I had heard about the release of ChatGPT. I hadn't, as over the Christmas break I had taken a break from work and all things work-related, including LinkedIn, so I had no idea what he was talking about. At first, I didn't know what he was referring to, so he explained briefly that it was an AI chatbot that generated high quality, human-equivalent copy, and promised to send me a link to download it after the meeting. He kept his promise, and I proceeded to download it and try it out for myself.

My initial reaction was this is not as good as a good human copywriter, but equally, it is better than a bad one! Like many copywriters, photographers, graphic designers and other creatives, I felt slightly threatened in the beginning and worried about the impact this would have on my livelihood. Had I effectively become redundant overnight? Would those happy to just have basic OK copy replace human copywriters with an AI chatbot? Was I one of the latest victims of creative destruction? Or could I use AI to my advantage? To find out more, I started to follow news stories about AI and posts on LinkedIn in which people were discussing it and generally joined the conversation.

One of the things that struck me was the similarity between the impact of AI on the copywriting industry and the impact machine translation has had on the translation industry in recent years. Specifically, it has sped up workflow, increased productivity and enabled translators to handle larger volumes of work. In my opinion, AI chatbots have done, and will continue to do, the same for copywriting.

I have decided to see AI as an opportunity, not a threat. So, over the past six months, I have learnt to use AI and have refined how to train it by entering the correct prompts. Think of it like a client brief. Just like I outlined earlier the importance of a detailed brief to enable relevant copy to be written, I have invested time in effectively briefing ChatGPT to ensure it generates the best response which needs the least editing. I no longer feel threatened by it and embrace it as a time-saving tool, and so should you if you want to be ahead of the competition or at least keep up with it.

Creative destruction: what is it?

I mentioned creative destruction as a concept earlier; this is a term my husband introduced me to circa 2008 when he was doing his degree in Computer Science and AI. As this section is dedicated to AI and the future of copywriting, I thought it only appropriate to ask ChatGPT to define what it is. One thing AI chatbots are good at is scraping the internet for information and summarising it in a concise manner, unlike a traditional Google search where you are presented with many different articles. Here is the response it generated:

Question posed to ChatGPT3:

What is creative destruction?

Response generated by ChatGPT3:

Creative destruction is an economic concept coined by economist Joseph Schumpeter. It refers to the process in which new innovations, technologies, or business models disrupt and replace existing ones, leading to the transformation and restructuring of industries and economies. It involves the simultaneous creation and destruction of economic value.

According to Schumpeter, this process is a fundamental driver of long-term economic growth and progress. Innovations and entrepreneurial activities continuously introduce new products, services, or methods that render previous ones obsolete. This dynamic forces companies and industries to adapt, innovate, or risk being left behind.

Creative destruction can be seen across various sectors and industries, where new technologies or business practices disrupt traditional models. For example, the rise of e-commerce has transformed the retail landscape, leading to the decline of brick-and-mortar stores. Similarly, advancements in digital streaming have disrupted the traditional music and film industries.

While creative destruction can lead to job displacement and economic upheaval in the short term, it is believed to drive long-term innovation, productivity, and economic growth. It paves the way for new opportunities, promotes efficiency, and allows for the emergence of new industries and markets. However, it also requires adaptation and resilience from businesses and workers to navigate and harness its potential benefits.

Let's now look back through history and consider some examples of creative destruction: in the Middle Ages, illuminated manuscripts were made redundant by arrival of printing; it was felt portrait painting would be ended by photography; yet calligraphy, illustration and portraiture are still with us but have adapted and changed. And now, here we are with AI chatbots pervading multiple industries. Each time new inventions have occurred, jobs have been lost and people have had to retrain but we still need humans; the only difference is the type of work that they do.

When I was growing up my mum was a secretary and PA, and her daily tasks included: typing, when she first qualified in the 1960s with a typewriter, and then later with a PC; answering the phone; sending and receiving faxes and letters; diary management; filing and other general administrative tasks.

Nowadays, many busy business owners, me included, have virtual assistants to help with our admin processes. They are essentially undertaking the same tasks but using different technology to do it - a laptop has replaced the typewriter; email and folder management as opposed to drafting and replying to physical letters, faxes and filing cabinets. Virtual assistants need a similar skillset to a traditional secretary: organisational skills; proactive, technologically savvy; time management and communication skills, etc. However, by harnessing technology, the mundane and repetitive elements are automated, leaving time for, yes, more creative activity such as creating presentations and actively managing contact data.

AI and its impact on translation

As a translator, you will be aware of how AI has transformed the language service industry in recent years with the increased use of machine translation using LLM (language learning models) and AI to do much of the heavy lifting for translators. You will also know that a machine-translated document still needs a human eye to edit it to ensure it reads fluently, is accurate and, ultimately, is publishable.

Depending on your specialism/s you will also know that it works better for certain texts, such as technical manuals where there is a lot of repetition and less ambiguity and need for emotive words. Texts of this type have long been able to leverage translation memories with terms such as "Open the flap", "Turn the knob to the right", etc. being very common and easy for AI to manage.

Conversely, more literary and creative texts still rely heavily on human translators, especially marketing texts which need to resonate with the target audience and require knowledge of the culture and norms of the local audience. As we discussed in Chapter 2, knowledge of history and culture, in addition to the target language, is crucial. That is when it is often best to utilise transcreation - a mixture of translation and creation, when the text needs to be faithful to the message of the source text but can be creatively rewritten as a marketing text. This is a way of ensuring that the salient points are translated but there is less need to be faithful to the source text in terms of terminology and structure.

One of the most entertaining AI-generated errors I have come across was in an Italian financial text that was explaining some new anti-corruption laws that had been introduced in Italy. The Italian source text read **Pene per il corruttore**, for which the machine translation output in English (the target language) was **Penis for the corrupter**! Of course, I knew this was incorrect, so after a quick chuckle, I used my human translation skills to correct this to **Penalties for the briber**.

Machine translation has come a long way, but can you imagine if the machine translated text above had been published without a human casting their eyes over it? As we know as translators, machine translation is fine if you just need to understand the gist of a text or for an internal company document. However, anything that involves publication in the public domain or people's lives or a lot of money, as in the case of medical and legal translation, still requires a human to edit it and to quality assure it to ensure accuracy, consistency and no faux pas, which despite making great memes, are not professional.

AI and its impact on copywriting

AI is now having a similar impact on copywriting, with many copywriters fearing for their jobs and wondering if their skills are still marketable in a post-AI era with ChatGPT and other AI chatbots seemingly doing their job for them. However, if you scratch the surface, AI chatbots, despite being very good at some things and undeniably faster than humans at writing articles, performing research and analysing data, lack the very qualities that make human copywriters essential: empathy, personalisation, knowledge of the client and their values, knowledge of the target audience, etc. In fact, all the things that we talked about in Chapter 6 remain relevant and set a human copywriter apart from an AI chatbot.

As I was writing this book, I thought I would ask ChatGPT what it thought the future held for copywriters and here is the response it generated.

Question posed to ChatGPT:

Will AI take over from copywriters in the future?

Response generated by ChatGPT on 2 July 2023:

The role of AI in copywriting is a topic of ongoing discussion and speculation. While AI has made significant advancements in natural language processing and generation, it is important to recognize that copywriting involves more than just stringing words together. It requires creativity, empathy, and a deep understanding of human emotions and motivations.

AI can assist copywriters by automating certain tasks, such as generating product descriptions or optimizing content for search engines. However, human copywriters bring a unique perspective, originality, and the ability to craft compelling stories that resonate with audiences on a deeper level.

In the future, AI may continue to evolve and become more sophisticated, potentially impacting certain aspects of the copywriting process. However, it is unlikely to completely replace human copywriters. The fusion of human creativity and AI technology is more likely to result in collaboration, where AI tools serve as valuable aids to enhance and streamline the copywriting process.

Ultimately, while AI may change the landscape of copywriting, the human touch and the ability to connect with readers on an emotional level will remain essential elements that AI cannot fully replicate.

As you can see, at first glance, ChatGPT3 writes well, with no spelling or grammar mistakes, but scratch the surface and you have the international Oxford English "z" spelling convention in "recognize" and "optimizing" and the use of the Oxford Comma (the practice of inserting a comma after the penultimate item in a list as in "*It requires creativity, empathy, and a deep understanding of human emotions and motivations.*" above). Depending on the style guide you are following or even your own personal preference it is not mandatory in British English to use the "z" spelling or the Oxford Comma, and yet, when

I asked ChatGPT to localise it for a British audience it changed some of the words but still used the Oxford Comma (see the comparison table on the next page). Of course, there are different conventions in British English such as Oxford English, which is most commonly used for international English purposes, and Cambridge English, which is generally the preferred convention in the United Kingdom. Your job as a copywriter is to ensure that any AI-generated copy is correctly localised for the audience you are addressing.

COPY THAT!

See the comparison text here, with the amendments made for a British audience underlined:

The role of AI in copywriting is a subject of ongoing discussion and speculation. While AI has made significant progress in natural language processing and generation, it's crucial to recognize that copywriting entails more than simply stringing words together. It demands creativity, empathy, and a profound understanding of human emotions and motivations.	*The role of AI in copywriting is a <u>topic</u> of ongoing discussion and speculation. While AI has made significant <u>advancements</u> in natural language processing and generation, <u>it is important</u> to <u>recognise</u> that copywriting <u>involves</u> more than <u>just</u> stringing words together. It <u>requires</u> creativity, <u>empathy and</u> a <u>deep</u> understanding of human emotions and motivations.*
AI can support copywriters by automating certain tasks, like generating product descriptions or optimizing content for search engines. However, human copywriters bring a distinctive perspective, originality, and the ability to craft compelling stories that deeply resonate with audiences.	*AI can <u>assist</u> copywriters by automating certain tasks, <u>such as</u> generating product descriptions or <u>optimising</u> content for search engines. However, human copywriters bring a <u>unique</u> perspective, originality, and the ability to craft compelling stories <u>that resonate with audiences on a deeper level</u>.*
In the future, AI may continue to evolve and become more sophisticated, potentially impacting specific aspects of the copywriting process. Nevertheless, it's unlikely to completely replace human copywriters. The fusion of human creativity and AI technology is more likely to result in collaboration, where AI tools serve as valuable aids to enhance and streamline the copywriting process.	*In the future, AI may continue to evolve and become more sophisticated, potentially impacting <u>certain</u> aspects of the copywriting process. <u>However, it is</u> unlikely to completely replace human copywriters. The fusion of human creativity and AI technology is more likely to result in collaboration, where AI tools serve as valuable aids to enhance and streamline the copywriting process.*
Ultimately, while AI may reshape the copywriting landscape, the human touch and the ability to emotionally connect with readers will remain crucial elements that AI cannot fully replicate.	*Ultimately, while AI may <u>change the</u> <u>landscape of copywriting</u>, the human touch and the ability to <u>connect with readers on an emotional level</u> will remain <u>essential</u> elements that AI cannot fully replicate.*

Using AI chatbots as productivity tools

Aside from the spelling and grammar issues highlighted above, it is important to note that AI recognises the value of human copywriters. A cynical, paranoid interpretation of this is that, well, AI would say that, wouldn't it? It's lulling us into a false sense of security before taking over the world, ha ha, but let's not get tied up in knots by that right now! Instead, in terms of the future of copywriting, in my opinion, it is crucial to view AI as a tool and a time-saving device that can speed up our workflow, make us more productive and efficient and enable us to serve more clients and generate more content. This is exactly what AI has done in translation where, due to the use of machine translation, we can now process larger volumes of work and consider ourselves more as editors and curators of content, providing that all-important human element that AI will never have.

As a copywriter, if you refuse to use AI you will likely find yourself falling behind the curve. Your competitors will become proficient in using it and will leverage its processing power to improve their productivity. So, I urge you to start using it and recognise it as just another tool to help you be, yes, more productive and creative in your copywriting.

What is prompt engineering?

Prompt engineering is the art of setting up your questions in ChatGPT so that you elicit the best response. Once again, as this chapter is focussed on AI and the future of copywriting, I thought I'd ask ChatGPT3 to provide some examples of prompt engineering.

Question posed to ChatGPT3:

Can you give me some prompt engineering examples in AI chatbots for copywriting?

Response generated by ChatGPT3 on 2 July 2023:

Certainly! Here are some prompt engineering examples for AI chatbots in copywriting:

"Generate a catchy headline for a new product launch."

"Craft a persuasive opening sentence for a promotional email."

"Write a compelling call-to-action for a landing page."

"Suggest engaging social media post captions for a clothing brand."

"Provide a creative tagline for a tech startup."

"Create a conversational script for a customer support chatbot."

"Generate product descriptions that highlight key features and benefits."

"Craft an engaging blog post introduction on digital marketing."

"Write a persuasive sales letter for a subscription-based service."

"Create compelling email subject lines to increase open rates."

These prompts can be used to guide AI chatbots in generating specific copywriting content. Keep in mind that AI chatbots can provide initial drafts or suggestions, but human copywriters should review and refine the generated content to ensure its quality, tone, and alignment with the brand's voice and objectives.

As you can see, these are basic examples of prompts. To go deeper and get the most detailed response, you need to explain to the chatbot all the elements that you would consider if you were writing the copy from scratch, such as the buyer persona, the target audience, the client's pain points, etc. If necessary, refer to Chapter 6 to remind yourself of the information you need to know before asking for a response to be generated. Effectively, you are feeding into the chatbot the detailed client brief you have created. As AI becomes increasingly sophisticated it will be essential to be proficient in prompt engineering to be able to maximise the timesaving, productivity boosting capabilities of AI.

Who AI-generated copy works well for

In my experience, any business owner who has no or little budget to pay for good copy, is not a professional writer, or who does not have strong written skills, or for whom the language they are writing in is not their first language, will hugely benefit from using an AI chatbot to generate copy. They will be able to produce blogs, articles, web pages, social media posts, etc. in the blink of the eye. The question is, can they also stand out from the crowd? Probably not. It is a low-cost option and, like most things in life, you get what you pay for.

For this type of audience, you could even choose to add 'AI-generated copywriting' as a separate service. You offer it to clients who you know, through networking for example, will not pay for bespoke human copywriting. Just as everyone is aware of the importance of social media as a business tool doesn't mean everyone uses it. Similarly, however wonderfully easy AI chatbots are to use to generate copy, many business owners will not feel comfortable or ready to use them. You will have invested time in familiarising yourself with their use, and for those owners of small businesses who you will never convince to use a copywriter, you can curate AI content for them, either 'mediated' (i.e., with a final edit by you), or 'unmediated' (WARNING: a penis may find its way into this text 😊).

How to edit AI-generated copy

If you are using AI-generated copy as an in-house tool, it should be treated as a first draft that you have produced or that your faithful copywriting assistant, keen to learn and improve their skills, has produced for you. Your job as a copywriter is very similar to that of a translator post-editing machine translation. You need to read it in its entirety, ask yourself if it matches the brief, and if it doesn't you need to edit it so that it has covered all the points mentioned in the brief.

Although it is unlikely that you will find many spelling or grammar mistakes you should localise it for your audiencee as discussed above. In my case, I would localise it using British terminology and spelling and grammar conventions. You will also need to personalise it for your client and ensure that it is consistent with their brand's tone of voice, their client avatar and that it includes the features and benefits of the product or service and that the buyer's pain points have been addressed.

Audiences are bombarded with information all day, every day and are becoming increasingly discerning about what they will and won't read and most people can spot poor copy a mile off, so beware, use it for idea generation or to get started but always apply your knowledge, creativity, judgement and empathy to AI-generated content before publishing it or sending it to a client.

Potential legal ramifications of using AI-generated content

AI and its ability to pervade so many aspects of our life, often behind the scenes without us even knowing it, in autonomous vehicles and medical diagnosis for example, means that there are various potential legal questions that have yet to be addressed. In the case of autonomous vehicles for example, who is to blame in the event of an accident - the passive 'driver' who is not controlling the vehicle; the manufacturer; or the company who provided the AI to power the vehicle? Introducing new regulations and laws is a notoriously long-winded process and the realm of AI is a fast-moving landscape with new applications being introduced daily so it will likely take years before the law catches up and regulates and legislates on the use of AI.

As a copywriter, you need to be careful about any claims that you make in your copy, particularly if it has been even partly produced by an AI chatbot. Fact checking is essential, as is checking for bias, discrimination and accuracy. If links are provided, make sure they are valid and to a site that you can trust. It remains unclear who will be liable in the future for false statements, inaccuracies and prejudice so make sure it's not you by being as thorough as possible when checking statements and facts claimed in your copy, whether you have used AI or not.

Final thoughts on AI

The things AI will always lack are emotion, life experience and the ability to use words to connect with people in the way that humans can. I think of it as a robot that lacks empathy but can process information and generate ideas faster than I can and, as I said above, you should treat it as a copywriting assistant and not a foe. It is only as good as the instructions you give it and, like machine translation, will cope better with more factual texts than abstract ideas and concepts which require human creativity, emotions and originality.

In the Oscar-winning movie *Good Will Hunting*, Robin Williams' character highlights to Will Hunting, the protagonist and child prodigy, that knowledge gained from reading alone does not have anywhere near the same value as knowledge gained from experience. When we were young, we learnt not to touch stinging nettles because we had touched one once out of curiosity and been stung. This experience taught us not to repeat the same mistake and means that we can empathise and sympathise with someone else who has been stung. The same applies to AI; it can spit out information at a phenomenal rate, but it cannot connect with people on an emotional level.

For me this concept is summed up perfectly in the famous 'Your move chief' speech from the film *Good Will Hunting*, which earned Matt Damon and Ben Afleck Oscars for Best Screenplay as they co-wrote it. In my opinion, this in akin to AI's lack of empathy, which is something that can only be gained by real-life experience. If you're not familiar with it, I recommend you look it up online.

COPY THAT!

Chapter 12
Cha-ching

"If you don't drive your business, you will be driven out of business."
B.C. Forbes

Managing two arms of your business

One of the things that I didn't foresee when I started offering copywriting was having to tweak the message I was sending to my audience, whether on social media or in my networking groups. As I mentioned in Chapter 5, after six months of promoting myself as a copywriter I felt that I couldn't talk about the translation arm of my business, as my virtual background (remember this was in 2020 during the Covid-19 pandemic when everything was online) only mentioned copywriting. So, I hired a graphic designer to create a Zoom background that matched my branding and clearly explained what I do so that even if I was on a call in which I barely spoke, people knew what I did and how to contact me.

Below is the Zoom background I currently use in all online work calls.

I therefore recommend that before you start trading as a copywriter you do the following:

- Edit your social media profile/s to reflect your new job title
- Create a landing page
- Create company pages on your social media accounts
- Update your website with a dedicated page to copywriting
- Rename or rebrand your company if necessary
- Create a virtual background that reflects your services
- Update your articles of association if you are a limited company
- Decide which service you want to prioritise in your marketing

If you don't get your own messaging right, you can't expect anyone to hire you to fix their messaging. Be clear about what you offer and what you want to achieve. Set income targets, track your leads and performance, and set measurable and achievable goals.

Watch the money roll in

The intention of this book is to provide you with an additional income stream by leveraging your existing writing skills and tweaking them to be able to offer copywriting as a service. If you have followed all the steps set out in this book you should now be ready to launch yourself as a copywriter and enjoy the benefits of having two income streams into your business.

Expect to start small and work your way up to bigger clients as your skills develop and your confidence grows. Remember to keep an eye on your pricing and put your prices up as your copywriting client base grows. You determine your own value and should charge accordingly. Unlike in the translation industry, copywriting rates vary wildly based on the skill and experience of the copywriter and the copywriter's ability to charge according to their value.

As I said in Part Five, for me one of the best ways to grow my copywriting business has been through networking. Now is the time to start researching groups in your area or online that you think could help you grow your business. Look for groups that can help you achieve your business goals and schedule and then visit them. Make sure that the other members are a good fit for your business and vice versa. Decide whether you would prefer to join a group with one member per category rule so that you would be the only copywriter or a group that welcomes more than one member per category. There are advantages to both. In the first instance you will be the go-to copywriter for the group. In the second, you will find opportunities for collaboration with copywriters that offer different copywriting specialisms and work in different niches. The main thing is that the group/s you choose to join can help you move your business forward.

Create marketing collateral such as a landing page, videos, a lead magnet, etc. for your copywriting services and start disseminating it on the social media platform/s that your ideal clients frequent. Remember to factor in whether you want to work B2B or B2C, as discussed in Chapter 8. You could start with a discounted price special offer to get started. Once you have written your first piece, request a review or testimonial to help build your confidence and that of future clients. Don't forget to talk about your reviews on social media.

You determine your own level of success

How successful you are will depend on how well you market yourself, as well as how good you are as a copywriter. You could be the best copywriter in the world, but if you don't tell anyone, or sell yourself, no one will know and no one will come knocking at your door asking for your services.

Unlike in the translation industry where you are assessed on tangible qualifications and asked to perform a test, many copywriters come from a variety of backgrounds, and the best ones may not even have a degree. **Fear not, you've got this!** If you have completed all the steps in this book you will now be armed with the copywriting and marketing tools that can move your business forward.

I hope you have enjoyed reading about my journey into the world of copywriting and have learnt some valuable takeaways for your business.

Tasks to complete

1. Start using ChatGPT and other AI chatbots to write a blog, strapline, article or website copy

2. Ask the chatbot to regenerate the copy using relevant, targeted and specific prompts, and note the differences

3. Localise, personalise and add empathy to the copy, as appropriate

4. Create a virtual background for online networking and client calls that lists your services and contact information

5. Write a landing page for your new copywriting service

Final words

Before I conclude this book, I want to add a note about its title. When the book was in its conceptual stage at the end of 2022, a Ukrainian refugee, whom my brother was sponsoring, stayed with us for a few days over Christmas. Whilst he was here, he responded to every piece of information about his stay that we gave him, such as "The fridge is there, help yourself to anything you want" or "If you go down into the kitchen at night, please shut the door after you so that the cats don't come upstairs and wake us up" by saying, "Copy that". After the first day, we all found ourselves saying it and it became a great catch-all phrase to respond to a variety of instructions or statements.

Once I had determined to start writing this book, I needed a working title. I played around with a few ideas and then, one day, it just came to me: *Copy that!*. I didn't know if it would stick, or if I would think of a better title, but in the end it stayed. I like it because it has a double meaning - without the exclamation mark it means "understood", but with the addition of the exclamation mark, "Copy that!" becomes an imperative and therefore an instruction as opposed to an affirmation.

Considering that the book is intended for translators, language professionals or other business owners who want to learn how to add copywriting as a service the title seems apt as I'd love you to replicate the things I have done to help you grow your own business. This book is my way of answering the question of how I went from being solely a translator to a translator and a copywriter. **It's all in this book and if you want to do the same thing, copy that!**

COPY THAT!

About the author

Antoinette Chappell has been passionate about language and communication her whole life. This passion extended to learning foreign languages after her first trip abroad, to Spain, at the age of seven and remained with her throughout her school years and steered her choice of degree. In 1996, she was awarded a BA (Hons) in Modern Languages from The University of Westminster.

After completing a PGCE at University College Chichester she went on to be a French and Spanish teacher before deciding to embark on a career working from home as a freelance translator to fit in with her family's needs. To do this, she enrolled on the Masters in Translation course at the University of Surrey, which she completed in a year and passed in 2007 with a distinction.

She has been working as a translator from Italian, French and Spanish into English since 2007, specialising in legal, financial, technical and marketing texts. She has also been a member of the ITI (Institute of Translation and Interpreting) since 2006 and, in 2014, she passed the ITI exam in Italian into English and now holds qualified member status (MITI).

In 2019, she decided to add copywriting as an additional service by leveraging and adapting her finely-tuned writing skills for a different purpose. Antoinette networks extensively to market her services and has built strong relationships over the years with other business owners and entrepreneurs, both nationally and internationally.

She now runs a London-based company called ARC Writing and Translation Services. She lives in Sussex and has two grown-up children and two stepsons and shares 3 grandchildren with her husband, James.

Follow Antoinette Chappell on LinkedIn and feel free to subscribe to her 'Word up' monthly newsletter, with insights and tips on copywriting and translation.

Recommended reading

- *The E-myth* by Michael E. Gerber
- *Obvious Adams* by Robert Updegraff
- *Building a StoryBrand* by Donald Miller
- *Atomic Habits* by James Clear
- *Advertising Headlines That Make You Rich* by David Garfinkel
- *Networking Like a Pro* by Ivan Misner
- *The 29% Solution* by Ivan Misner
- *Ogilvy on Advertising* by David Ogilvy
- *Strengthsfinder 2.0 from Gallop* by Tom Rath
- *Wired For Story* by Lisa Cron
- *The Copywriter's Handbook* by Robert W. Bly
- *Copywriting Made Simple* by Tom Albrighton
- *Storytelling for Business* by Rob Wozny
- *The 1-Page Marketing Plan* by Allan Dib
- *The Micro-Script Rules* by Bill Schley
- *Webs of Influence* by Nathalie Nahai

COPY THAT!

Bibliography

Chapter 1

Writing styles: https://www.grammarly.com/blog/types-of-writing/

Strengthsfinder 2.0 from Gallop by Tom Rath

Chapter 2

UK consumer trends: https://www.askattest.com/our-research/2023-uk-consumer-trends-report

Chapter 5

Obvious Adams by Robert Updegraff

Ogilvy on Advertising by David Ogilvy

Building a StoryBrand: Clarify Your Message So Customers Will Listen by Donald Miller

Chapter 6

Advertising Headlines That Make You Rich by David Garfinkel

Endnotes

1. Gen Z are considered to be born between 1997 and 2012.

2. Boomers are considered to be born between 1946 and 1964.

3. AIDA stands for Attention, Interest, Desire, and Action. It is used in copywriting to structure copy, as each term represents the stages of the customer's buying journey.

4. *Obvious Adams, The Story of a Successful Businessman* by Robert R. Updegraff

5. *Building a StoryBrand: Clarify Your Message So Customers Will Listen* by Donald Miller

6. *Advertising Headlines That Make You Rich: Create Winning Ads, Web Pages, Sales Letters and More* by David Garfinkel

www.ingramcontent.com/pod-product-compliance
Lightning Source LLC
Chambersburg PA
CBHW071345080526
44587CB00017B/2966